W9-AZM-680

The
Dirty Guide to
WINE

The Dirty Guide to Wine

Following Flavors from Ground to Glass

Alice Feiring

With Pascaline Lepeltier, Master Sommelier

THE COUNTRYMAN PRESS
A division of W. W. Norton & Company
Independent Publishers Since 1923

For information about permission to reproduce selections from this book, write to Permissions, The Countryman Press, 500 Fifth Avenue, New York, NY 10110

For information about special discounts for bulk purchases, please contact W. W. Norton Special Sales at specialsales@wwnorton.com or 800-233-4830

Manufacturing by Versa Press
Book design by Anna Reich
Production manager: Devon Zahn

The Countryman Press
www.countrymanpress.com

A division of W. W. Norton & Company, Inc.
500 Fifth Avenue, New York, NY 10110
www.wwnorton.com

978-1-58157-384-8

10 9 8 7 6 5 4 3 2 1

FOR OUR MOTHERS, EARTH, AGNÈS, AND ETHEL

Nor indeed can all soils bear all things. By riversides willows grow, and alders in thick swamps; barren mountain-ashes on rocky hills; on the seashore myrtle thickets flourish best; and the god of the vine loves open slopes as yew trees do the freezing north.

—Virgil, *The Georgics: Book II*

CONTENTS

Contents

Pacific Northwest
Volcanic

California
Sedimentary
Volcanic

Canada
Limestone

East Coast
Sedimentary
Metamorphic
Granite

Chile
Granite

Major Bedrock Types
in Winemaking Regions

France
(see detail
below)

Germany
Schist

Austria
Gneiss
Loess

Greek Islands
Volcanic

Galicia
Granite
Schist

Georgia
Sandstone
Limestone
Volcanic

Rioja
Gravels

Italy
Sandstone
Limestone
Granite
Igneous
Shale

South Africa:
Granite

Australia
Granite
Limestone

Champagne
Chalk

Beaujolais
Granite
Schist
Limestone

Loire Valley
Granite
Schist
Limestone
Sedimentary
Flint

Alsace
All major soil types

Jura
Limestone

Burgundy
Limestone
Clay

THE RHONES:
Northern Rhone
Granite
Schist
Limestone

Bordeaux
Gravels
Limestone

Southern Rhone
Limestone
Gravels

Languedoc
Schist
Limestone

FRANCE

FOREWORD: THE DIRTY WORD

By the gods, Socrates, I am lost in wonder (thaumazô) when I think of all these things. It sometimes makes me quite dizzy.

—Plato, *Theaetetus*

As usual, we were late and rushing to the next appointment, driving fast through the barren January Anjou landscape. Alice was next to me and friends tasting with us were in the back. We had just left one appointment at a manor carved out of the rock that made the region special: yellow tuffeau limestone. The wine we tasted there, grown on that white and jaundiced soil, was from Chenin Blanc. It was dancing, lingering, salty, timeless. But just a few miles away, where we were headed now, the landscape changed from limestone to schist. I told the girls in the back of the car, "We are entering the dark side, the Anjou Noir."

Within minutes, we were in a garage cellar, tasting a Chenin from the very slope we had driven down. So different from the earlier one, this Chenin was powerful and tannic and just as lively, if not more. That schist had to have something to do with it. One afternoon. Two sensitive, vignerons-gardeners with their micro-vineyards, two transparent Chenins. Two expressions of their place: Anjou Blanc and Anjou Noir. By that point, Alice and I had tasted so often together we didn't need words. We looked at each other and knew what the other was thinking: "There you go. Proof again of the beauty and the reality of dirt."

Dirt was probably why Alice and I got along right away—and the genesis of this book can be found in our first meeting, ten years ago. It was in Paris in 2007, during a tasting organized by low-intervention vignerons, Patrick Desplats, Jean-Marc Brignot, and Julien Courtois. I was playing the sommelier and Alice was there to taste these very naturally made wines.

All in the room were like-minded and believed that a real wine could only be produced from vineyards carefully observed and taken care of with no synthetic chemicals, where the vines were in tune with the biodiversity around, so the plants could produce the best possible fruit. The vinification would not need any trick, just a wise assist from the vigneron, to produce an honest wine that would change in every year as the season changes every year.

The first wines I shared with Alice expressed all of these elements. Every wine I have cared about since was viewed in that way. Dirt has become a fascinating way of discovering the world of wines.

When I decided to become a sommelier, I went through rigorous professional training. I was taught to approach wines analytically. I learned the facts and data behind the different appellations and grape varieties; I practiced deductive tasting to recognize the structure and the aromatics, to identify the technical faults; I received templates to facilitate grasping the wine world's complexities. And, indeed, knowing all these things left me with a certain feeling of security—for a short time.

The feeling of safety ended when I realized the tools did nothing to help me understand the wines I was the most attracted to. Those analytic criteria were condemning the bottles I cared about because they were not the norm. Wines were segregated into camps, using some ideas developed by the French philosopher Bergson, on the mechanical side. That's where brix + min % + pH + etc. = wine. Yet, to me, on the organic and the natural side, the wines that I considered alive could not be quantified by sums of parts. These wines needed to be taken as a whole; the fundamental cell division, with its own inner balance. So, after all of that training, I was not prepared to "analyze" these types of "alive" wines that left me deeply amazed, puzzled, and astonished. And so it appeared that a lot of that wine world was full of ideas and concepts not appropriate to grasp what they were talking about, leading to false problems, like the hot topic right now of "minerality." Minerality has become a dirty word par excellence.

In a society reliant on reductionist thinking, the link of dirt to the glass has come under attack. The pundits call this minerality, and it is a false problem.

There's no minerality in wine.

One cannot taste the small oyster shells, *Exogyra virgula*, in a Chablis or the taste of basalt in wines from Mount Etna.

But yet, even if the scientists and the technical wine people tell us it isn't so, that doesn't mean that a sense of place doesn't get delivered and that dirt and soil don't have a part in it. Even if no one really yet understands "how" this can happen. Science is a work in progress trying to understand the "vital impetus", within the limits of our mind.

So this book is not a scientific one, and even less an anti-scientific book. It is not a geology nor a geography book. This is not a book to give proof that you can taste rocks in your wine. It is an emotional one in the way that the only wines worth drinking are emotional.

No, instead *The Dirty Guide to Wine* is an invitation to taste the wine world through new landscapes and new perspectives; an invitation to connect places and bottles, through the looking glass of the soils derived from their underlying bedrock. And please do understand that often the word soil is used here as a shorthand for just that. It is supposed to make you ask even more questions, open the taste buds to new experiences. The more we wrote the book, the more we knew what we did not know. We can not bring any answers, as all of the vignerons who we met and talked with were puzzled, and indeed amazed, by the relationship between the vines and the wines. They were all humble and aware of their lack of understanding of such mysteries, even as their experience grows. The fascinating and always changing synergy between a grape, a terroir, a vintage, a man (or a woman) captured in a bottle.

One summer day, thanks to Alice's recommendation, I found myself in Tbilisi, Republic of Georgia. This trip was to greatly change my vision of wine—as part of everyday life and not only as a luxury commodity— and my approach to tasting. I had the most unusual, thought-provoking experience. My host, painter, vigneron, cook, and singer John Wurdeman, was attempting to realize a lingering idea he had developed while traveling the different regions of his adoptive country: to experience synesthesia. Through rhythm, tonality, and structure between the local dishes, wines, and song of six major provinces of Georgia. And there we were, guinea pigs feasting over five hours with our ears, palates, and brains. Two typical dishes were served, two or three traditional wines made in *qvevri* were poured, while a couple of men were singing polyphonic songs, the patterns and vocabulary of which were unique to that territory. It was too overwhelming, and my extremely limited knowledge of Georgian culture limited my ability to understand. But I felt a connection, and I could not deny the possibility that synesthesia, or terroir in that case, could be experienced in songs or wines or food. That day I realized how much intuition and amazement could enlarge my vision, and my pleasure. That tasting was an incredible catalyst for this book: Just because the invisible wonder of the dirt can't be seen, and its influence on the vines and the wines can't be formally and decidedly quantified, doesn't mean there is no connection. And if we can't understand it yet, we can already appreciate it and stand for it.

I can't thank Alice enough for taking me with her on this journey, provoking me to think and taste differently. It is a rare blessing, and a real curse, to be a free spirit nowadays—yet she fights the right fight.

I am beholden to her for all the conversations and discoveries that happened throughout these pages, as I am to all the vignerons who opened bottles and thoughts and welcomed extraordinarily stimulating exchanges of ideas, not only making me a better taster but also someone more aware than ever of her place and responsibilities in this world—a duty to be amazed.

—Pascaline Lepeltier

INTRODUCTION

"The wine world has been held hostage by grape variety for nearly three decades," the editor and publisher of *Wine & Spirits* magazine said to me one night, over drinks.

He was right. Only recently had people started to march up to the bar and say, "I'll have the Chardonnay, please." Before the 1980s, few people cared about what the grape was called; they drank Burgundy or California table wine. The name-the-grape frenzy emerged from a new crop of winegrowers who wanted to create a market for their Cabernet and Shiraz. Soon thereafter we started seeing bottles that touted their grape name, rather than the region they came from.

"So what are you going to do about it?" he asked, not quite kidding.

"Well, as a matter of fact . . ." I answered. I realized I had already started to write this book, at least in my mind, several years beforehand, when I was in northern Alsace at the stellar restaurant Le Bistro des Saveurs. Not surprisingly, their wine list was as thick as a Larousse dictionary. The surprise was in its organization. The well-curated bottles included a huge selection of local wines. They were categorized not by the village or region nor by their grape name. They were categorized by the kind of bedrock the vines were planted in—limestone, granite, basalt, schist, etc. If I wanted to compare two Rieslings grown in basalt soil, the choice was mine. And what's more, I could compare it to one from granite and marvel at the differences and the power that different soils held over a grape.

That brilliant list crystallized an aspect of modern wine drinking that had bothered me for a long time: Consideration of the type of bedrock and topsoil a grape vine is grown in has become almost mocked in the mainstream wine world, yet it is essential to the way the wine tastes and ages. The type of soil a vine grows in has a profound effect on the resulting wine's taste. That knowledge deepens the thinking person's drinking enjoyment.

If only I had understood wine when I was in college as I do now, I would have gotten far better grades in earth science class. But growing up with only a small patch of backyard and not being much of a nature girl, the idea of rocks forming and transforming over eons seemed too abstract. It all changed when I started to traipse through vineyards and discovered the various ways that soil, history, and place affected wine. Then and only then did a soil's evolution begin to have meaning for me.

The more I thought about it, the more excited I became. Here's why: I want to give the drinker a whole different way to relate to wine. I want to release drinkers from choosing a wine solely on grape type. After all, if you're convinced the only wine you want to drink is Cabernet Sauvignon, how could you ever discover the wonderful wines from places that don't grow it? Not to belabor the point, but the point begs for belaboring: For centuries it wasn't Pinot Noir, the wine was called Beaune. It was not Cabernet; it was a wine from Napa. People never said they wanted Tempranillo; they wanted a region in Spain, Rioja. Until very recently a wine's place was far more important than the grape.

Don't get me wrong: The type of grape a wine is made from is important. Different grapes have very different qualities and not all soils are suitable to all varieties of the vine. But if wine is going to grab you and suck you into its mysteries, knowing where it comes from and what kind of soil and rock it grows in adds so much more intimacy to the drinking. If you limit yourself to drinking only by grape you lose out on a lot of wines that don't fall in the little box you've chosen for yourself. Take the state of Vermont, with its complex mix of igneous, sedimentary, and metamorphic soils. Deirdre Heekin, whom I consider to be their finest grower, is experimenting in order to discover which grape varieties work best there for the winery, La Garagista. She favors hardy grapes called hybrids, the likes of Marquette and the oddly named Louise Swenson. The results have been astounding. If you thought of yourself as only a Merlot or Chardonnay drinker, you might miss out on the licorice-like former and the honeysuckle-like latter.

I asked her to speak a little more about the connection between the soils and her experience:

> Granite, marble, and slate are the state rocks. The Rock of Ages quarry in Barre is the largest granite quarry in the world(!). Down near Ascutney, which is a dead volcano, there is a lot of lighter colored granite and gneiss. I forgot to mention gneiss too! Yes, there is gneiss. We have gneiss in Barnard. So the major ones you find all over Vermont: limestone, granite, quartzite, gneiss. There's also calcium from limestone and other calcareous bedrock. That's what makes Vermont soils sweeter with better pH than New Hampshire or Maine, which are naturally more acidic. The calcium helps raise the pH while also improving the breakdown of organic materials in the soil allowing the plants to better absorb the mineral nutrients. It's one of the reasons why I think it's so exciting to grow wine here. You see the direct, symbiotic relationship between plant and mineral.

Over the past few years the very notion that soil mattered—the notion that was held sacred by the ancients—has been challenged by scientists, pundits, and reductivist thinkers. Part of their game has been to take on a descriptor—minerality—used to describe a certain edge. This has been confused with an old-fashioned term, *goût de terroir*. Esteemed food writer Harold McGee found that the phrase started to change in the early 19th century. The change is evident when the father of Australian wine, James Busby, wrote in his 1825 book *The Treatise on the Culture of the Vine and the Art of Making Wine* that "The taste of the soil, *goût de terroir*, is frequently a virtue, as in that called gun flint, *pierre de fusil*, and sometimes disagreeable, as when aluminous. These latter and many other tastes in the wine are inherent in the nature of the soil; and it is to this that many delicious wines owe their peculiarities."

So does the vineyard geology go directly into the glass? Or is that the magical work of the wine writer who romanticizes their descriptors with poetic and not scientific license?

In a 2008 research paper, geologist Alex Maltman wrote, "The notion of being able to taste the vineyard geology in the wine—a *goût de terroir*—is a romantic notion which makes good journalistic copy, and is manifestly a powerful marketing tactic, but it is wholly anecdotal and in any literal way is scientifically impossible. Thus critical evaluation leads to the conclusion that the role of geology tends to be exaggerated."

What I disagree with is this argument about a phrase that was never supposed to be scientific, but evocative. Exaggerated? Perhaps. Over-romanticized? Perhaps. But irrelevant? No. Impossible? No. But within the scientific community there is dissent. In a recent interview with *Science Life*, Professor Jack A. Gilbert, who studies how microbial communities assemble themselves in natural and man-made environments, indicated the bacteria which a vine is exposed to—originating in the soil—could influence the flavor and complexity of the wine in subtle ways by affecting the chemistry of the grape.

He was talking of soil, others were talking about rock, but how can they be seperated? I used to make fun of winemakers who told me to lick their rocks. But the more I got into soil, the less absurd it seems. For years I've used descriptors like silver water, blood, and iron in my tasting notes as a positive. These are all qualities that seem to me to be of the earth and never of the grape itself. I cannot prove myself wrong or right—and frankly I have no desire to. What I do know is that fruit and vegetables are inexorably linked to the soils they grow in.

In a blind tasting, some of the well trained can actually ascertain some soil flavors. One of the easiest is fruit that comes from heavy clay, where there's usually a chunky quality. Granite? There is often something about texture. Limestone? The quality of the acid comes through. Grow Pinot Noir on limestone and on granite in the same exposition and climate, you'll get two different ripenings of the grape. You'll get different sugars and different acid structures, different longevity, and that translates into different tastes. Take this further and some can definitely ascertain an ashy finish from wines on basalt-derived soils or a rusty nail component in wines from soils rich in iron.

But while discussion of how and whether the tastes of the stone get into the wine is endlessly debatable, it is not the point of this book. Rather, this book is a way to organize learning about wine. Want to explore my favorite places in the world that have granite as a base? Done. The best places for limestone—and what grows on those soils? Done. Dirt is aiming at place and the soil—the foundation for any superior wine.

When I talked about writing this book, my colleague, Pascaline Lepeltier, MS, asked whether she could take part. I didn't have to think twice about accepting her help. An ace student with a talented palate and a like-minded wine drinker with a similar ethos, she always is bringing back rocks from wherever she goes. In short, she's obsessed with soils and organic viticulture and minimal winemaking. Neither one of us has to be convinced of the importance of the soil. We are of the same mind that not all places are created equal.

So, finally, here is a guide that we hope helps lead back to what is important. Taste the wines and come to your own conclusions, but as one must know that milk comes from a cow, as one likes to know what their chickens are fed, it is useful to know where and in what the vines lay down their roots. I am not a geologist; neither is Pascaline. This is not a geology book, though be prepared for a few words on the subject.

This book offers a different way to learn about wine. Not by region. Not by grape. Not by Old World versus New World, but grounded in the soil and place first. And then? Sure, after we have established the groundwork, bring on the grapes. After all, they are the vehicle for us to experience some truly amazing places.

THE BASICS OF SOIL

What is soil? This deceptively simple question needs some exploration before going forward, because it's not just about dirt. One of the most common mistakes—and guilty as charged—is to use the word soil to really talk about the defining bedrock. But they are completely different. Soil, and this is topsoil, is the covering that cushions the Earth's hard rock, which is bedrock. Its origin can be from the sea or from volcanoes, from plants, trees, leaves, rocks, animals, and microorganisms. Over the eons, organic and mineral matter erodes and decays. That soil is home to fungi, bacteria, worms, and other critters. It is where they conspire to extract the minerals needed for life. They deliver them to the roots of the plant, the plant develops, it finds its way to our table and nourishes and feeds us—that is, if that soil is alive and not destroyed by intensive agriculture.

Topsoils manifest in a range of textures, including sand, gravel, and clay, and consist of multiple layers. The top is the organic matter humus, the rich nutrient layer that can be deep, shallow, or non-existent. Just below that is the mineral subsoil, made of eroded rocky bits from the bedrock and decomposed organic matter. This is also called the clay-humus complex, and that's where the magic happens between the roots and the soil. It is where the plant takes in necessary nutrients—such as nitrogen, phosphorous, potassium, calcium, magnesium, iron, and boron—for its metabolism. Underneath that is the parent material, which can be the rock that defines the region, though—and this is important—it is rare that one region is ever 100 percent one rock type such as schist or granite. Underneath that layer is the almost impenetrable bedrock that in a few thousand years will become soil.

It is essential to the vine, to the plant, and to humans that the soil remains vibrant, full of activity and life, as it is the basis for everything that happens next. Soil has often been called the planet's skin, but when I heard someone say that the soil is the planet's gut, it seemed even more profound.

You'd have to live under a rock not to have heard about the importance of gut bacteria. Just as we have healthy bacteria that live in our intestines, healthy soils, such as the ones from the winemakers in this book, have up to a staggering 100 million to 1 billion molecules of bacteria in one little teaspoon. That's a lot of life. What does that mean to the vine? Soil scientist Patrick Holden sees it like this: Those microbes play a central role in breaking down organic matter into absorbable nutrients, which are then available to plants through their root systems. Another noted microbiologist, the soil guru Elaine Ingham, remains dismayed by the many lingering mysteries: "We know more about the stars in the sky than about the soil under our feet."

While some people need scientific proof, others go with their gut. But sometimes all you need is a visual. Take a walk into a Champagne vineyard, as I did with a friend in 2003. It was a long time ago, but vineyards in the region for the big companies haven't changed much. We stood in the vines of Pierre Larmandier; the soil was spongy and bursting with life. Just next door were vines belonging to Veuve Clicquot. The Clicquot soils were compact, unyielding, and barren. The juxtaposition of dead and living was enough to change my friend's relationship to her table and drink choices. On an emotional level, she understood the difference and from then on could taste it in the glass. She wasn't going to drink industrial champagne ever again.

TOPSOILS AND TEXTURES

Often it is the texture of the topsoil—clay, sand, gravel, silt, loess, or loam—that defines a region.

CLAY: When we talk about clay, we think of the dry stuff that gets slippery when wet. But if you dig down into the molecular particulars, clay minerals form in sheets. This structure has a huge impact on the way the clay functions. Some say that there are certain clays that are better for pottery than vines, but that's hotly contested. It depends on where you are, what your climate is, what kind of wines you want to make— blowsy or elegant—and what clay minerals are in the mix. And when you get a certain amount of the right stuff, like in Burgundy, where clay is mixed with limestone, it can be just what the climate ordered. The important aspect about clay is its plasticity and its ability to expand and contract with water and hold on to those minerals, saving them for the plant's digestion.

When clay dries, it shrinks and hardens on the surface. But deep down, the clay subsoil holds on to the moisture in its tight little fist, generously doling it out to the thirsty soils during drought conditions. Can you taste clay's effect? Some sure can. Look for a richness in the middle palate, sometimes a rustiness, and sometimes a deep cherry that you know does not come from the vine. The taste can feel blocky in the mouth. The terroirologist Pedro Parra says that these wines are more generous and rounder, providing the exception, because in this soil you do feel fruit. Some examples of areas that really stick to your

Blundstone boots and show the wine in your mouth: Abruzzo in Italy, Imereti in Georgia, Emilia Romagna in Italy.

SAND: Whether it's a beach carpeted with white silica or a shore spread with black grains of basaltic glass, sand is a texture, not a rock. It can be made of anything that is pulverized. Unlike clay, sandy soils drain easily, like a sieve. This is a boon in a monsoon-like season. But in a drought? Pity those poor vines, unless they happen to be planted in an especially humid climate. Still, most old vines still standing on their own roots are on those sandy patches of vinelands throughout the world. Can you taste the sand's effect? In 1825, influential wine aficionado James Busby wrote that "the sandy soil will, in general, produce a delicate wine." But it could also produce a simple one, especially if on very beachy sands of silica, and often gives a direct translation of fruit flavor that makes for uncomplicated but fun presentations, as if there is nothing in between the grape and the taste. Some great examples are from the sedimentary Californian Evangelho Vineyard outside of Sacramento (look for labels like Bedrock, Dirty & Rowdy, Sandlands, and Dashe) or the Colares region in Portugal. On volcanic sand, this would be Mount Etna in Sicily and Lanzarote in the Canary Islands.

GRAVEL: These rocks, ranging from pebbles to cobbles, are mostly associated with sediment and limestone. The rocks easily absorb the heat and as a result contribute to making more alcoholic wines which, depending on where this is, could be a bane or boon. Lesser known are the Gimblett Gravels of New Zealand and Walla Walla in Washington. Some extremely famous regions are Châteauneuf-du-Pape and the Médoc and Graves sections of Bordeaux.

The most exalted gravel soils in the world come from Bordeaux. This region has a curious history which reaches back to the 17th century, when the Dutch drained the swamps on what was then unusable land. In doing so, they exposed alluvial beds and plenty of gravel. Gravel, whether pebble-size or boulder-size, was extremely beneficial in getting the hard-to-ripen vines of Bordeaux to give tasty fruit. Why? Sure, gravel gives great drainage, important in the often-wet Graves region. But primarily, when the gravel is light in color, it is about warming the earth, about reflecting the sun and holding onto the heat. Whether limestone or basalt, texture and size trumps the mineral component of the gravel. Often the land is so difficult to farm, it's not suitable for anything else but vine.

SILT: Sometimes called stone dust, silt is finer, more fertile, and has better water retention than sand. But in farming one has to be careful as the soil is prone to compaction. Not exactly the best soils for grapes, but great for clogging up your water pipes.

LOESS: Caught between silt and loam, loess is made up of chiefly wind-blown sediments, mostly silica. You find it referred to widely in Austria, where they rarely grow their Riesling on it. In Walla Walla, Washington, it is quite deep, like a layer of sawdust, and very well drained.

LOAM: While not literally a texture, it is a combination of textural elements. Fertile (and sometimes too fertile) loam is a pretty even mixture of sediments: sand, silt, and clay. This combo is at home in much of California, where, compounded by the state's fertile soils, one has to expect a great deal of fruitiness. If you consider that the best wines are said to come from poor soils of low fertility, well, draw your own conclusions. That said, one can make smarter farming choices based on climate. What could work? Increase competition in the vineyard by growing the right vegetables between the rows and adjust the trellising of the vine. So all does not have to be lost!

WHAT MAKES A GREAT VINEYARD SITE, AND THE CONUNDRUM OF TERROIR

I was standing with Aubert de Villaine, the managing director of the iconic winery Domaine de la Romanée-Conti (DRC). We were in his parcel of La Tâche, a Grand Cru in the village of Vosne-Romanée. As we stared at the soil, he mused about the veracity of the superiority of certain spots: "Do you need science to prove the sun rises?"

We all know this intuitively, but de Villaine has the advantage of decades of observation. The most sublime recognized plot in Vosne-Romanée, and perhaps all of Burgundy, is one that DRC takes its name from: Romanée-Conti. And when I ask him what makes a great spot, he cites that one: "Out of all of them, it deals with the weather conditions the best." In the end, what makes a great terroir is the mixture of all of the elements together, where you have to do the least, where the vines are at peace and not in conflict.

There are some undeniable truths to certain places, no matter what science says on the surface. It is entirely possible that with two adjacent pieces of land farmed using the exact same practices, one of them will prove better than the other. Why? It's complicated, but each place has a unique microclimate drawn from the hyperlocal factors of wind and weather, as well as minute differences in an area's propensity to frost, hail, and humidity. And some places just seem blessed.

Terroir is a lot of things other than soil. But it is the soil that gives the vine a fighting chance.

So what are the best soils? It's not easy to categorize. Often, scientists get it wrong. Take a situation a few years back, when a friend of mine, Andy Brennan, wanted to make cider in New York's Catskills. He found his preferred spot, but the folks at Cornell told him that shale was terrible for apples. He almost believed them until he realized his location was crawling with wild fruit and had a centuries-long apple heritage. What were those agriculturalists thinking? He bought the place and the cider continued. His Aaron Burr Cider is tops. A great farmer has intuition and uses it, no matter what the scientists say.

Most sites have their charms, provided you plant wisely to their specifics. Whether limestone, basalt, or schist, as de Villaine says, "A great terroir is not too little and not too much. It is a soil that helps the vine through the other elements." One can say the same thing about a human life. To de Villaine, a great soil is part of the total picture. It is at best a place to grow that is not prone to difficulties, where one does not need to irrigate, and where one can do as little as possible to nurture grapes. It is a spot protected from warm winds if the land is in a hot zone, or protected from cold winds in a cold climate. The best soils are in places where nature is most in balance.

THE RIGHT KIND OF FARMING

Grapes are sensitive on one hand and sturdy on the other. The saying goes that you need to plant them where nothing else grows. That makes sense, because the grape vine can grow on the tops of volcanoes, on rock or ash, or in sand. Since they are so resilient, why give them the same soil in which you can grow corn? It's the concept of no pain, no gain. Make life too easy for them and you'll end up with a dumb fruit. But make them struggle to go deep into the ground in search of a drink, in soil that is poor? Now you're talking. But civilization likes things easy. So in comes unnecessary irrigation, bad for the environment and fine wine alike. In come the earth-moving machines to flatten the land. In comes chemically-enhanced farming. Out goes quality.

Almost all of the winemakers in this book make the point repeatedly that topsoil can be trumped by the farming. Mistreat great topsoil and you'll get crappy wine. Treat dubious land beautifully and thoughtfully, and be prepared for a good surprise. Pierre Breton, at this point a legendary winemaker (with his wife Catherine) of Bourgueil in the Loire, says that "if one thinks soil affects the taste of the grape and the acidity, it is only because when you work without chemicals in the vineyard you bring the rich humus, which creates more microbiological life to the soil." His point is that if the roots stay superficial as they do with ultra-modern methods, you get superficial tastes. In listing different producers throughout this book, I have included their farming philosophy and whether or not they are certified.

So what are the options to working the topsoil?

CONVENTIONAL: This is a pleasant way of saying the farmer used herbicides and pesticides. They may or may not plow, but probably not. No one who farms this way is in this book. If there's one polemic in this gentle book it is this: Chemically intense farming and additive winemaking is totally against our philosophy and occludes the place where the vine is grown.

SUSTAINABLE: Okay, so this one is like being a little bit pregnant. But there are all variations of sustainable. The French call it *lutte raisonée*, which is farming by common sense. Basically, it means "we reserve the right to spray when we need to spray." Some people never pull the trigger. Some spray all the time. So how do you know if the farming is real? That's the problem. Everyone lies. It's sad but true. So you have to rely on people like Pascaline and me, who visit a lot and ask the hard questions.

ORGANIC: In this approach, the farmer says ix-nay to all synthetic chemical herbicides and pesticides but does treat for disease using organic preparations. Back in the '70s, the organic farmers were made fun of as hippies who made ugly-looking vegetables. Today this more conscientious approach is spreading like crazy. We are now in the era of industrial organic, which is at least better than no organic.

BIODYNAMIC: Developed by the philosopher Rudolf Steiner (1861–1925), this practice borrows pages from the ancients and takes a spiritual and homeopathic attitude toward farming. In biodynamic farming, you pace your practices to nature's rhythms. You work to understand the art of transformation through natural processes like fermentation, maybe by burying cow dung to turn it into pure and potent compost. Common practices include vineyard treatments that are organized according to the season, locations of the constellations, and the phases of the moon. The object is to heal, not harm. It is proactive rather than reactive. Its scope in farming is far greater than just the physical dirt and vine. This farming is based on nine treatments that are of animal, vegetable, or mineral origins, sprayed in homeopathic doses. They seem to really work, though the ingredients raise snickers among the detractors. Dung, nettle, silica, and chamomile, for example, can be made into teas that are dynamized by intense swirling in water. This fosters a spiritual and hyper-observant bond between the farmer and the vine, and this in and of itself cannot be a bad thing.

NATURAL FARMING: Whether you're a follower of permaculture or a follower of the cult of beloved Japanese farmer Masanobu Fukuoka, the idea here is the same: Do as little as possible. Use the ecosystem to do your work for you. Use beneficial plants to bring nutrients to the soil. Plant herbs like clover that will aerate and open up the soil instead of using invasive plowing. Take a natural approach to the vine, understanding that the vine is in balance with itself, that in the wild the ecosystem heals all. For more on truly do-nothing farming, take a look at the Hirotake Ooka profile on page 83.

THE RIGHT KIND OF WINEMAKING

Most people are stunned when they learn that most wines out there are not 100 percent grape. The truth is that there are about seventy additives that are completely legal for winemaking. But it is my heartfelt belief that the only wines that truly manage to communicate place and vintage are those that start with at least organic viticulture and then have only grapes, with perhaps minimal sulfite addition. In other words, real wine generally has nothing added and nothing taken away.

The alcoholic fermentation process is the same in all grapes: Yeast gobble up the sugar in the fruit and produce mostly alcohol, plus carbon dioxide. There are a few ways of accomplishing this. The most common is to crush the grapes and let the yeast soak up the sugar. The other is to put the grapes, still whole, into a covered vessel, pump in CO_2, and allow the fermentation to start inside the berry. This method of fermentation, called enzymatic, combined with various kinds of carbonic maceration, became identified with the Beaujolais region and now is often used to make easygoing, fragrant wines. All choices along the way impact the flavor and the color of the wines. The most basic choices are:

- How will you farm: conventional, organic, biodynamic, etc.?
- Will you harvest the grapes by hand or use machine picking?
- How to sort the grapes: on a special sorting table (maybe even one that vibrates)? In the field?
- Destem grapes or keep them in bunches with stems intact?
- Make wine with whole bunches or just using whole berries?
- Crush by foot, vertical press, or bladder press?

- Remove grapes from their skins immediately or choose skin contact?
- Add the preservative sulfuric dioxide (SO_2) and in which dose or proceed with none?

Wines come in all sorts of colors and textures. The color usually comes from the length of time the wine is fermented on the skins. White wine usually starts from white grapes like Chardonnay. However, white wine can also be made from pink grapes, like the pink-skinned Pinot Gris or red grapes, like Pinot Noir, as long as the flesh itself isn't red. Rosé is a blush-colored wine, made from either a blend of red and white (especially in the Champagne region) or with just a few hours of skin contact on the grape. Amber-colored wines (sometimes called orange wines), meanwhile, are made from white or pink grapes with quite a bit of skin contact, from hours to months.

Then you have to decide what sort of container you want to put the wine into. Whether it's glass, fiberglass, stainless steel, cement, clay, or wood, you'll have your pick of different sizes and shapes. Wood choices? There are plenty: oak, cherry, acacia, chestnut, etc.

If using an open-top fermenter, which is true for most reds, a crust of grape skins forms on the top of the fermenting wine and you must push this "cap" of grapes under the liquid. This is done by machine, plunger, grid, or feet. You do this to keep the cap wet and safe from bacterial infection. This also extracts color and tannins, so you don't actually want to do it too much.

Once fermentation naturally starts, it can take a couple of days or months to finish. As the mixture ferments, it gives off carbon dioxide.

When alcoholic fermentation is finished, even if there's some sugar left over, the juice has been transformed into wine. It might have even gone through a secondary process called malolactic fermentation. That is when bacteria turn the harsher malic acid inside the grapes into the softer lactic acid. This rounds the wine and naturally stabilizes it, and is far more common in red wines than white. You may or may not change the vessel and leave the wine there until it tastes ready. In making red wine or amber wine, once fermentation is finished, or when the color and extraction desired is achieved, it is time to press the wine off from the skins.

The next decision is whether to remove the dead yeast cells or not. This might sound weird, but the leftover yeasts create a kind of silt, called lees, that actually has a lot of beneficial properties. The decision to remove them is often made in pursuit of a very clean flavor. But when you do leave the yeast, this is called *sur lie* aging. It is often used in Muscadet to give richness; when stirred, as is often done in Burgundy, the lees can impart a creamy, almost oaky flavor to the wine. This stirring is called *bâtonnage*. The lees gives a certain protection to the wine as well, so it's quite useful when making wine without sulfur. Many natural winemakers choose to keep a wine on the lees.

So what are the different ways to make wine?

CONVENTIONAL: Allows any and all of the above. Winemakers are also allowed to use extreme machinery such as reverse osmosis, dialysis, or thermo-vinification, all of which affect and homogenize the final product. The upper limit of total SO_2 allowed in wine in the US is 350 ppm (parts per million); in the EU it is 160 ppm for red wines and 210 ppm for dry white and rosé wines.

CERTIFIED ORGANIC WINE: All additives labeled organic are allowed. All processes are allowed. In the United States, no SO_2 addition is allowed. In the EU, there are various laws governing organic wines; for SO_2 addition, the maximum for reds is 100 ppm and for dry whites and rosés it is 150 ppm.

CERTIFIED BIODYNAMIC: This certification is not governmental but provided by private associations such as Demeter. In the United States, Demeter allows 100 ppm SO_2 addition. Some additives might be allowed, including added yeast, by petition. Biodynamic wines from Europe adhere to stricter rules: the maximum for reds is 70 ppm, and for dry whites and rosés it is 90 ppm.

NATURAL WINE: There are no official laws governing this method, but it is presumed that it includes natural farming and a winemaking philosophy of nothing added or taken away, except maybe up to 20 ppm of SO_2. Many natural winemakers choose volcanic sulfur instead of the petrochemical derivative sulfite, which is the norm.

What's the Deal with SO_2?

Sulfur dioxide (SO_2)from volcanic or petrochemical origin is commonly used as an additive in winemaking for its function as an anti-bacterial and anti-oxidant. Its use is ancient, dating back to the Romans burning sulfur dioxide inside of amphoras to sanitize them. With the modern age, SO_2 was used in the process of winemaking for further control. A certain amount of SO_2 is naturally produced as a by-product of fermentation, but, because it's an allergen (although other additives like tannin are probably worse), the bottle must carry a cautionary label if a wine has more than 10 ppm. Natural winemakers believe that the harm done to the wine—it binds it up and they believe it contributes to hangovers—is worth avoiding. So, in desiring to deliver the most expressive and healthy wine possible, avoid SO_2 except in minute amounts.

CAN YOU REALLY TASTE DIRT?

How many times have I tasted with a winemaker who swears that the flint aroma in the wine comes from the silex in the soil or perhaps declares that the ginger quality in a Meursault comes from the soil's limestone? I've lost count.

It is nearly impossible to link up specific soils to tastes. If we claimed that was possible, Pascaline and I would be Twitter-shamed by the wine community so fast, it would be a social media wildfire. And they would be right. It just ain't possible. However, there are a few benchmarks, and you can train your palate to look for them.

Soil has an impact on the delivery and quality of acids and tannins. We can't overstate enough that weather and farming choices, as well as technique in the winery, have huge impacts as well. For example, a hot, sunny year brings higher alcohol and what is referred to as a solar wine. Wood aging can bring out the flavor of tannins. Using whole bunches of grapes adds a certain spiciness.

So why all of this emphasis—a whole book!—on soil if we can't give you a direct correlation? Because looking for the clues from the soil, even if you don't find them, heightens your tasting sensitivity and increases enjoyment. And more than anything, it brings you, as a drinker and wine lover, back to where the root of your passion resides—in the soil. It's just like how knowing music theory boosts your emotional response to a Beethoven sonata higher than you thought possible.

To listen to where a wine comes from, pay attention to acidity, saltiness, and tannins, the basis for its texture and structure. The aromatics are interesting but not as important, as they are constantly changing.

Wine pros talk about vertical and horizontal structure. These give shape to a wine.

Different wines hit the mouth in a variety of ways. Some give you a very long finish, meaning the taste goes on for a long time. Some seem to wash over in your mouth, and you might feel it across your tongue from left to right; that is horizontal.

Wine pros also talk of a wine's acid structure. While that sounds a bit complicated, questions of acid structure are all about where the zing hits in your mouth: On the top? Near the tip of the tongue? In the back of your mouth, toward the throat?

Another characteristic pros talk of is tannic structure. This is about the raspiness, much like the tannins in tea or coffee. They can come from non-wine ingredients such as wood, but in a natural wine, tannins come from the grape skins, stems, and seeds. The tannins can be harsh and green, or grippy, dry, wet, fat, and even chalky. Sometimes I use the word needle-like, because they feel like a narrow line drawn through the wine. Sometimes the sensation is just a mouthful of broad tannin that goes all over the place.

Not to get too New Age-y about it, but take a breath and take a moment to notice it all, from the beginning, middle, and end of a sip of wine.

Another term wine pros yammer on about is dry extract. You can visualize this somewhat off-putting term this way:

Take a drink of filtered water, and then drink a bit of highly mineral-laden bottled spring water. You'll taste the difference. You'll feel a touch of celery salt, something rusty or coppery, some briny characteristics, some grit. Now try a glass of Muscadet, the elixir-like wine from the western Loire. You should pick up the same sensations and aromatics as the mineral water.

To further visualize what we mean by dry extract, leave a couple of drops of wine in your glass on the counter of your kitchen overnight and look at the bottom of the glass the day after. You should see a white film left behind after the wine has evaporated. It seems to be an extract of the wine itself. Is it grainy to the touch? Is it salty to the taste? Think back to the mineral water, to the Muscadet. That's it.

All of these characteristics might be able to give you clues to a wine's native soil. Try to be aware of them before you just settle into drinking, as they might help you to connect the dots later on. It will be easier for you to taste the difference in white wines, as they are the most transparent. So in your tastings, try to go in the order of white, rosé, sparkling, amber (perhaps), red, and then, finally, sweet.

AOP, AOC? What do they mean?

Most countries have ways of certifying wine districts and their wines, but the French formalized the concept in 1936. This was the Appellation d'Origine Contrôlée, or AOC. This system, which is now called AOP, was developed in order to inform the public what lands are considered better or classier than the others, calling attention to the specific characteristics of that place and that wine. This started as an attempt to control fraud and ensure what was claimed to be in the bottle really was in the bottle. It became the industry standard in Europe, and other countries followed suit.

The Italians have a DOCG, which stands for Denominazione di Origine Controllata e Garantita and is the most exalted, followed by a DOC. The Spanish have their DO system with DOC, Denominación de Origen Calificada, at the top. In Portugal there is a DOC/DOP. The Greeks have the PDO (previously called OPAP and OPE). In the New World, the Americans have their AVA, American Viticultural Areas, of which Napa Valley is one, as is its subset, Oakville AVA. But unlike the laws of Europe, there are no laws governing how to make the wine, what grape varities are allowed, where the vines should be planted, or what kind of wines are allowed to be made from the specific region. This is partially thanks to the New

World notion that all grapes can grow anywhere, but in the end, the category is more about political, administrative, and financial interests than any extraordinary regional or soil qualities.

An appellation can be a large region such as the Côtes du Rhône, or a micro one, such as Cornas or Saint-Joseph. It can denote one particular vineyard with special qualities, such as Château-Grillet, or it can even be a kind of wine, such as Clairette de Die, which is an as yet not wildly popular Rhône sparkler. Those in charge of the regulations outlined the rules with a peer group of producers for each individual region, determining what was allowed to grow, where it was allowed to grow, and how large the yields could be, as lower yields are associated with higher quality. In some areas, such as Bandol in France, Rioja in Spain, and Barolo in Italy, there are even laws about how long a wine must spend aging in wood, tank, or in the bottle. Because of the EU, what was previously known as an AOC has been changed to AOP, meaning a protected appellation, which stretches across EU borders. As of 2016, it is still confusing, but hopefully will be slowly accepted over the coming years.

Meanwhile, there is dissent in France, the country from which all of this regulation originally sprouted. Over the past 20 years, the INAO—the board that governs the appellation rules—has been under attack. Some believe that what had started as a protection has now become a danger. The association has gone into the business of legislating not just what and how to grow but how a wine should taste, based on preconceived notions of what is popular in the market, rather than respecting local traditions and subscribing to the well-tested attitude of "*vive la différence!*".

It's rather dangerous to think of wines that are sound and yummy yet outside the box as deviant. This could open the gate to much manipulation in the winery. All winemakers are motivated by some idea of commerce. Is a grape that is low-yielding and highly acidic, one that is not for everyone, really a grape that should be allowed? This kind of attitude has allowed situations like that of Romorantin, booted out from everywhere in the Loire except one little tiny village, Cour-Cheverny. But even more disturbing is the belief that the organization has elevated commercial wines over truly artisanal ones. Often it has rewarded commercial and cookie-cutter wines but shunned wines of personality. This has led to a defection of some very fine producers who've chosen a 'lesser' wine label, such as Vin de France or Vin de Pays or Vino di Tavola (table wine), for freedom. The trouble with these labels is that it is forbidden to print the exact location where the wine comes from. And to me, that's almost the most important detail when I make my decision about what wine to buy. Place matters. Period.

HOW TO TASTE WINE

First, you'll need a glass.

Forget the paper cup. It really is better in a glass. I prefer a glass with a very thin rim, and I don't care about the bowl, it just needs to be big enough for the wine to breathe. Please note, however, you should avoid very wide mouth glasses, like the champagne coupe, as too many of the aromatics will be lost.

Then you want to drink.

Very early on, one learns manners when it comes to food—how we should eat with a fork and a knife or keep our mouths closed when chewing—but are we typically taught how to enjoy wine? Naw. Just drink. But then there are those times someone shoves a glass in your hand and says the dreaded word: "Guess!" So in that case, what do you do? You look, swirl, sniff, sip, swallow, and, like a detective, look for clues. Clues are everywhere. Here's the way Pascaline and I handle it.

GIVE IT A QUICK FIRST SNIFF: Certain aromas disappear very fast, especially if you frantically swirl what's in your glass. These are the lightest, most delicate whiffs. They whisper to you about the wine's nuances—leaves, flowers, fruits. Grab them before they vanish and never come back.

LOOK FOR CLARITY: Is it cloudy? That could mean the wine was not filtered nor fined. These are processes, chemical and physical, that can polish a wine and remove floating particles. But that doesn't mean that a wine that eschews these methods is always foggy. Take for example the Georgians, who make their wine in buried amphoras and leave it untouched for up to eight months, after which it goes into the bottle absolutely clear. So just look, notice, and don't judge.

LOOK AT THE COLOR: White, red, rosé, amber? Look carefully from the core to the rim. Generally, white wines get deeper in color with age, while red wines get lighter. Young whites have a green or silver hue, young reds a pink-purple one. Amber-colored? It could be old and poorly stored, or it is a lovely wine from white grapes with some skin contact during the aging or fermenting process.

LOOK AT ITS TEXTURE: Give the wine a swirl. Look at the way it runs down the side of the glass. Those are called "legs." Thick drips correspond to higher alcohol content. When they cling to the glass you can pick up clues to the wine's origins and the vintage. A thinner wine should come from a cool vintage or climate and viscosity from warmer ones. Depending on how syrupy, the wine could be rich and sweet. Not much grip on that glass? Then it might be a cool-climate wine. No legs at all? Well, then your glass is too clean. Try again. Now, is there crud floating in it? Don't worry, that's harmless. The wine could be old and that's sediment—some people insist that drinking it keeps you healthy. If the gunk looks like crystallized sugar, these are called tartrates. The wine develops them if not filtered and if it has been kept cool.

SMELL FOR PROBLEMS: Some people think anything out of the ordinary is a flaw, but truly sometimes all a wine needs is time. Here's what is going on. Is the wine corked—meaning, does it smell like a musty cellar or a long-dead animal? It could be because the winery or the cork was contaminated with a compound called TCA (2,4,6-Trichloroanisole). This is not a good thing. Or does it smell like a small closet stuffed with live sheep? We might have a problem with a strain of yeast called *Brettanomyces*. A little bit is not so bad, but a whole flock is an issue. Does it taste like pure and sharp vinegar—enough that it hurts your nose? In this case, there are severe problems with acetic bacteria; in other words, the wine has turned to vinegar. A little scent of nail polish remover? That's called volatile acidity, and as long as the wine tastes agreeable and is in balance, it is not a problem.

SMELL FOR PLEASURE: Look for fruit and or savory aromas, and have a good time with your nose in that glass. Not all wines have strong aromas of fruit like grapefruit or mango or elements that came out of a perfumer's suitcase, so open up your mind as well as your nasal passages. If the fruit is way too vivid and sterile, the wine's fermentation might have been kicked off by yeast, instead of relying on the natural stuff. Or it was made with extreme temperature control or in a stainless steel container. If the white wine is savory, it could have been raised in concrete or clay pots of some kind. Can you smell the vessel it was made in? These aromas may include vanillin, cherry vanilla, burnt toast. When the aromas (and flavors) keep on coming at you, then you know you have a complex wine in your glass.

SMELL FOR SERVING IT TO YOUR GUESTS: If you're having a dinner party, you need to open up the wines to figure out if you need to decant them. So take a smell. Notes of boys' locker room, rubber, or struck matches? That means the wine is probably reduced—meaning it's been kept without oxygen and needs to breathe. Certain grapes like Syrah are prone to it. Certain winemaking practices or closures, such as screw cap closures, foster it. What about little bubbles in a still wine? That's fine. Some winemakers who make wine without the pre-servative sulfur trap the CO_2 during fermentation in order to give the wine protection (it displaces oxygen, which degrades the wine). But if it's more than a little stinky and the wine is supposed to be a still wine, plunk the wine into a decanter or a pitcher. Many wines need a bit of this oxygenation to open up; thus, the real reason for serving wine from a decanter instead of the bottle.

TASTE: Now you get to confirm your suspicions or confound them. Is the wine dry or sweet? Fruity or savory? Alcoholic or gentle? Old or young?

Notice the wine's structure, what some call its bones. When tasters use words to describe what they like, such as big, rich, tannic, light, sparkly, and fresh, they are talking about that skeleton.

Some wines have no bones. They are sloppy, flabby, and have no point of view. At the other end of the spectrum, some are like a slash or a punch. And some are well-mannered, with a distinct beginning, middle, and end. Ask yourself: Is the wine flabby? Does it have a bright-ness? Does it burn with alcohol? That might mean a high acid red with some grippy tannins that probably hails from a northern climate. That exuberant, rich white with a pear-skin, bitter almond, tannic quality is probably a thick skin white from hot-summer region.

SPIT: I always thought I'd never do this in public. Hah! The first time I was in a room with 100 zinfandels to taste, I knew I had no choice. To taste a wine when spitting is involved, you look at a wine, draw it in, aerate it a bit as if you're slurping soup, bring back a little in your mouth, feeling the roughness from tannins (or the sweetness or the bitterness). You'll also be able to smell additional aromas through something called retronasal smell, which uses the back door to your nasal passage. Then spit it out in as beautiful a spit as you can manage. Even if I don't have 99 more to go, tasting a wine this way helps me focus on the wine's component parts.

DRINK: Any way you like. After all, this is the point.

Some people (like Pascaline) can taste wines and zero in on the vintage, the grape variety, place of origin, and sometimes even the winemaker. Some people—like Raj Parr, a sommelier and winemaker—can damn near get the kind of soils the vine grows in. This is rare and extremely difficult. But the most important thing you're looking for is whether or not you like it. And if you like it, you can start to bring your tasting up to the next step, considering how you can serve the wine, what to pair it with, and how long you can keep it for. That is where you start and finish. The rest is for the professionals and for party tricks.

In 2016, I was asked to chair an award for naturally made wines at the Vin Italy wine fair. I brought Pascaline along to be one of my five judges. Most awards are given on points, with a certain amount of points given for color, aroma, clarity, and taste. But I presented my own criteria to the judges, and they worked very well indeed:

LIVELINESS: At first sip, there is a lift in the mouth. This could be related to a nice acidity.

EVOLUTION IN THE GLASS: The wine is not locked into place, but might reveal something new with every sip.

BALANCE: There is the sense that all is well in the glass. The elements— even those that could be seen as flaws in conventional wine, such as *Brettanomyces*, volatility, and even some mousse or reduction—are all in harmony.

DRINKABILITY: You would like to drink the wine. This gives pleasure.

EMOTIONAL IMPACT: Can a wine make you feel? Of course it can. It can make you recoil in horror. On the other hand, a wine can make you smile, laugh, and feel intrigue and excitement. Even if there is a negative reaction initially, the first impression of the wine can be improved by it having any number of the other qualities.

SAVORY QUALITY: A wine can be pure fruit juice and be pretty, but it should also have an element of savoriness, evoking dried herbs, leaves, forest, pot, fresh hay, leather shoelaces, olive, Earl Grey tea . . . and so on. These flavors can often elevate a wine to greatness.

TRANSPARENCY: Is the wine a block? Is it impenetrable or can you see through it? Can you tell its details, something about the way it's made? Does it seem honest to you? Can you tell the vintage detail? Can you hazard a guess as to whether it was made in a warm or cold year?

SENSE OF PLACE: Finally, there's that terrific elusive quality. Can you tell where you are in the world when you sip it, even if you are wrong? Does the wine take you somewhere?

In my book, if you have any six of these, then you've got an award-winner in your glass.

CHAPTER 1

IGNEOUS

How can you not be captivated by the idea of making wine from the roiling, boiling, sulfurous, belching belly of the Earth? I am obsessed with these igneous soils, especially those born of the volcano. And more often than not, I find I am drawn to wines that come from them. At first, this seemed like an accident. But then, as I delved deeper into the taste similarities, I began to wonder if it was so very random. Volcanic wines have a very specific texture; sometimes it's an ashiness, sometimes it's an edge or what terroir expert Pedro Parra would call a "nervous sensation."

These igneous soils have a parentage of magma, the molten, fiery, subterranean blood of the Earth. But how the magma manifests itself—whether it stays beneath the surface or whether the lava bursts out of a volcano's crater—informs the kind of rock it becomes. The resulting stone is either intrusive rock or extrusive rock; fraternal twins of the same parent, but with different gestational conditions. Intrusive rocks mean that they are formed inside the Earth under pressure and heat. This includes the boulders that the volcano purges, as well as the heated, cooled, and pressurized Earth that becomes gabbro and granite. Extrusive rocks come from lava flows that cool and harden outside of the womb, on the Earth's surface. The lava takes centuries to degrade and become arable soil. The rocks that are formed in this process include: rhyolite, pumice, tuff, scoria, volcanic ash, and, most importantly, basalt.

BASALT

The extrusive, iron-rich basalt is made when hot lava flow cools. The best examples are found on islands.

Basalt is complicated. It first occurred to me that it was one of the most intriguing soils when I was visiting the Canary Islands, one of the most profound spots of volcanic activity in the world. Just off the North African coast, belonging to Spain, almost all of these islands have a wine history, some more volcanic than others. Lanzarote and one section of La Palma have black, ashen soils that squeak as if walking in ebony snow. To think that a vine could squiggle down underneath to find rock and mineral in a soil almost absent of clay seemed death-defying. All I could think of with certain wines I had from there was, "Basalt, straight from the Earth's iron core to the glass."

Shortly after that fabulous trip, I traveled to Washington State to give a talk on terroir at Whitman College. Lo and behold, my host Kevin Pogue was a basalt specialist. The forces were sending basalt messages to me. During the downtime, Professor Pogue ferried me around to see some of the local Walla Walla basalt-derived soils of the Columbia Basin.

I shared with him my newfound passion and asked him how it was possible that basalt was so ignored in the wine world. He said that for one, not a whole lot of wine areas have vines planted on it, and yes, basalt was a little miracle.

Basalt can hoard magic inside its form. There's even some research being done about soil amelioration with basalt dust and exploiting its water-holding capacity, especially vital when so many vineyards around the world are facing drought conditions due to climate change. The professor kneeled down, picked up a black rock, and set me straight.

The rocks he showed me are assets to any cooler vineyard—radiating warmth, promoting ripening. Because lava cools quickly, extrusive rocks such as basalt are fine-grained. But it is when the hard material breaks down into well-drained soil that the impact on taste can start. Battered by rain and heat, the rocks weather into coal-dark or oftentimes red soil. Why red? Iron. Think about a nail exposed to water: It's the same thing. Coming from the Earth's core, these stones were filled with iron, which, whether in soil or man, impacts energy. We know that too little iron in our blood leads to anemia and loss of power. Too much of it beats a path to toxicity. Just the right amount turns you into Popeye. In the vine, iron is also necessary. It is an essential nutrient in photosynthesis and aids chemical reactions. Pogue noted that iron has also been shown to affect the composition and concentration of the phenolic compounds responsible for aroma and flavor.

"But," he said to me, speaking like a scientist, "what we don't know is how these elements affect smell and taste in wine."

Whether true or imagined, I sense a particular soil, a rusty, edgy ash with almost oxidized acidity, in some of my favorite basalt-grown wines. Whether or not basalt will ever go head-to-head against other terroirs, like limestone or granite, in terms of noble status remains to be seen. But if you're looking for examples of the quality basalt can produce, a few places have already distinguished themselves.

Mount Etna

Are Etna wines as popular as winemakers there believe they are? Is it the hand of a marketer or promoter, or is there some truth to the hype? Those were my thoughts as Pascaline and I stared, mesmerized by the smoke plume that constantly puffs out from Mount Etna's mouth, which they call La Contessa. Just in case we thought about relaxing too much, La Contessa was a constant reminder that the volcano never sleeps and that she was the real boss of Mount Etna.

The majestic Etna is screwed down on the northeastern part of the Italian island of Sicily, constantly belching and puffing. It's rich in mystique and mythology. The deadly monster Typhon, it is said, was buried deep within. According to Greek mythology, this was also the mountain where the Cyclops roamed and collaborated with the gods' blacksmith, Hephaestus, to create Zeus' thunderbolts.

With all of that godly history, no wonder there's so much ego on the mountain. But while ego speaks the loudest, the best work speaks humbly. Etna has only been bottling its wine instead of just making wine for immediate consumption for 20 years or so. Historically, they made their wines in *palmentos*, a series of old cement bath-like cisterns. Just as every country house in Georgia has their tiny *marani*— the place dedicated to winemaking—almost all rural houses on Etna had a *palmento*. However, in 1991, the EU, in all of their determination to turn Europe into a soulless mall, outlawed these multi-level stone troughs where the grapes were stomped, supposedly because they're not sanitary enough. And so now the new way is stainless steel, new wineries, and a loss of the very device that made the local vintage unique. So why is this little piece of heaven in Sicily in this book if the wines aren't completely formed yet? Because underneath it all, this place has climate, soil, and grape. The potential for brilliance is huge.

The Dirt

There was no better tour guide to the Etna dirt than viticulturist and winemaker Salvo Foti. He has been the keeper of the history and authenticity of Etna. We spent a day going to his vineyards, from the lowlands to his highest vineyards—1,300 meters up, far higher than the region allows him to make a DOC (short-sighted of them). There, we stopped to chat to a neighbor who just pulled out some wild onions and greens from the ground for his dinner. "The dirt is fertile and rich, but the basalt is also sandy, fine sand, dry with very little if any clay," says Foti. And in that is yet another paradox of the soil: fertile but poor. That is what gives the wine its tension.

To work the land there is difficult. Black basalt stones are plentiful. The big companies employ earth-moving machines to level the land and the soil. But among smaller farmers, painstakingly working the soil—often with hoes, as if they were in a Bruegel painting—is common. Foti has been the major proponent of continuing to grow the vine in what is called *albarello*, where one vine is strapped to a single chestnut pole instead of strung on a wire in more conventional trellising. This also is tough. "It takes two hundred days per hectare to work this way, instead of fifty," he says. But it's worth it because the grapes get even more nourishment from the plant, and thus the grapes ripen evenly on the vine.

Through the vineyards we visited with him, we saw black volcanic ash similar to the kind I saw on the Canary Islands of La Palma and Lanzarote, where they call it *picon*. Several times a year, Etna spews forth a torrent of blue-black ash that covers cars, chimneys, and vineyards. It doesn't greatly affect the terroir, but it's a constant reminder that the volcano is no joke. Pumice also gets spat out of the caldera. These light, porous stones in black and gray, textured and airy as coral, are more relevant to the terroir. Pumice helps to absorb the water that falls on Etna, nourishing the vine. Meanwhile, Pascaline filled her pockets with dirt and rocks to take home.

There's another trick to working the soils: a moat dug around each vine. Some people say this is Foti's idea, but Foti says he is just reviving an old way of farming: "This helps to focus the rain that does fall down into the roots of the vines." He also believes that this enables the plant to better access the minerals in the soil.

At the end of the trip, Pascaline tried to get through security with her six-pound bag of rocks. Stopped by the guards, she begged them not to confiscate the stones. They looked at her as if she were a crazy person. "Why do you want these?" they asked. Thinking quickly, she said, "I just want to take something back home of your beautiful country."

Winemaker Profile: Vino di Anna

Petite, spunky Anna Martens speaks fluent Italian with an Australian accent and is one of many newcomers to Mount Etna. Unlike many Etna winemakers, who insist they're the best, she keeps a low profile and has her own way of exploring the wines of her area. It also helps that she was a winemaker in Italy and in Etna before she laid claim to the land.

Martens was working in Italy when her husband Eric Narioo, a wine importer based in London, came to Etna in search of a flavor he had tasted in a bottle of wine made on the volcano. I understand the draw. That wine was made not in a traditional Etna way (because Etna, until recently, made wine primarily for quick drinking) but in a traditional Italian way, where sometimes a bottle will be aged for up to six years before releasing. It translated the basalt soil as an ashy, lively wine with character.

The impulse to follow a bottle often leads to a new chapter, and the couple decided to explore the territory. Anna started working as a winemaker for Andrea Franchetti's Passopisciaro

Vineyard. Seeing the landscape crawling with gorgeous abandoned vines, like shelter kittens that needed adopting, they decided to make Etna their second home and started to collect an assortment of stunning vineyards. Narioo took us to a truly special spot on the northern slope of the volcano. We stood high above where the eruption of 1981 came rushing down and ravaged the land.

Up in Eric and Anna's newest vineyard, there was an Alpine-like freshness. Pascaline and I stood there in awe with Eric during a spring when Etna was bursting with brilliant purple wild irises and cherry blossoms. Mount Etna looked like Mount Fuji. And looking down, we could see the lava that had frozen in its tracks after ravaging the vines. Only 30 years old, it needed centuries before it would degrade into soil. Standing in that vineyard with the meticulous terracing still intact, one could be intoxicated by the power of nature of the volcano. Looking down, mesmerized by the grazing animals below, Eric confessed that the real problem with Etna is conflict with the shepherds over who owns the land. Some of the stories of this clash rivaled those in *The Godfather* and included severed horse heads and terrible fires.

Perhaps because they are not from Etna, Eric and Anna have more of a sense of freedom. Foti, who works on their viticulture, planted some Riesling and some Chenin, taking advantage of the higher elevation and the crisp volcanic air. But freedom has its own price.

Flying between London and Etna with two small boys is not the easiest lifestyle. I asked Anna where her peripatetic energy came from? It's kind of like a surfer in search of the perfect wave, she said: "The volcanic soils have an amazing energy.

They're fertile and full of minerals such as copper, iron, and boric acid." Then there were the aesthetics, the tradition of vineyard cultivation with its dry-stone walled terraces and old *albarello* vines and the native grapes. Much like a musician looks for a glorious instrument, a winemaker is looking for the perfect grape in which to translate the soil and place. Anna viewed Nerello Mascalese, the region's prime red grape, as a wonderful vehicle to express the many nuances of Etna's terroir.

Calabretta, a traditional winery located on Etna's north slope, uses a variety of *botti*—those big old barrels—but the couple chose a different method of winemaking; a type of Georgian amphora called *qvevri*. Having been given a present of two of these giant earthenware pots, she experimented. She liked what came out of them and ordered more. On the property there was an old *qvevri* she rehabbed and uses for one wine as an "experiment." It's a lovely wine, very much like a *vin de soif*—wines for thirst. Just glug it back and have a good time. However, the bulk of her wines are a little more serious, even if they are made in clay pots. She hasn't totally abandoned wood, and often uses a combination of barrels, some older, some larger, some Slovanian, and some smaller, but never adding a woody flavor to the wine. Her wines will join other vintages like Calabretta's Etna Rosso—the wine her husband came in search of—and Vini Scirto and take Etna to a place that people will revere.

The Grapes

Nerello Mascalese was first bottled on its own here in Etna in 1985, but it took another decade for the wine's character to solidify. While it's now common, winemakers aren't quite sure how to make it or what to make of it. What it does have is structure and rasp with a core of blackberry. One quote that I think says it all is from grower Giuseppe Russo of Girolamo Russo: "Nerello has a unique capacity to express the character of the soil it's growing in; plant it anywhere else and it loses its soul."

There are a variety of ways on the island to discover its native reds— my five favorite producers use five different methods. Salvo Foti is reviving the art of making wine in the outlawed *palmentos* after pleading the case for the tradition in the EU, arguing that it was the lifeline of the people on Mt. Etna. He's set to work to resurrect the practice on his property and has just made a Nerello using foot-stomping and open basins. After raising it in old oak and chestnut, Foti bottled what he refers to as his illegal wine. Frank Cornelissen, who is rather obsessed with no outside flavors in his wine except grapes and terroir, destems, vinifies in fiberglass, then raises the wine up in epoxy-lined buried Spanish amphoras. He bottles it quickly, and the new vintages are usually bottled within seven months. Anna Martens (see her profile on page 56) is another clay vessel devotée. The Calabretta winery vinifies as they do on the mainland with traditional ferments, raising in old oak and chestnut barrels of various sizes, and then up to ten years of aging. And a very recent newcomer, Eduardo Torres Acosta from Tenerife, who is living in Sicily and making wine on Etna, brings a whole different approach. He takes his crop and combines three different vinifications: with stems, without stems, and crushed. Then the mixture goes into very old barrels.

For white grapes, the one to watch is the salty Carricante, an Etna Bianco high-acid grape, with citrus overtones that can truly age beautifully. Salvo is retiring in Milo, which is the only commune allowed to label its Carricante as Etna Bianco Superiore, with its view of the eastern side of the mountain and the Ionian Sea. The soils there are super sandy, with plenty of the pumice they call *ripido*, "stones from the sky." "Volcanic soils are sandy soils," Foti said. "There is virtually no clay in the soil." We tasted Foti's Carricante Aurora in the vines and then later in his winery, just a few meters away from its origin. Whoa, was it a beauty! I believe in the wisdom of Foti, but was Etna the only place it could gain glory? When Pascaline and I had a chance to have a wine which came from the Calderara contrada, the heart of Nerello country where Foti has his old vines, I realized life existed for the grape elsewhere. The wine was made by a young couple, Giuseppe Scirto and Valeria Franco, and at six years of age it had developed into a salty melon of a wine with nerve. It was rooted in soils similar to Foti's vintages, but from a warmer spot, facing north instead of facing east and the sea. While all eyes are on Nerello, we had to wonder: Was Carricante the real gem of Etna?

WHO TO DRINK

- I Vigneri (organic)
- Cantina Calabretta (organic)
- Vini Scirto (organic)
- Frank Cornelissen (organic)
- Vino di Anna (organic, biodynamic)
- Eduardo Torres Acosta (organic)

The Canary Islands

Closer to Africa than its parent country, Spain, battered by the winds and eons of volcanic eruptions, this collection of seven islands in the middle of the Atlantic has stayed a secret until quite recently.

All but one island make wine today, but if you believe Shakespeare and Kant, the Canary Islands were hot properties back in the 17th and 18th centuries. In fact, right up to 1797, when Lord Nelson lost his right arm (and several hundred men) on the Canary Island of Tenerife, it was the next best thing. But something happened over the next 200 years or so and the islands went unnoticed, until a Spanish ex-pat, US-based importer José Pastor "discovered" them and the Canaries started their comeback. There were two aspects that attracted the various wine snobs to the area:

1. In the late 19th century, a vine-sapping pest devoured much of Europe's grapevines. A grafting technique saved the industry but left the fruit altered, and certain tastes were lost forever. Or so it was thought. It turns out the pest never infested the Canaries. The vines there, grown in volcanic soils, are a direct link to a distant winemaking past.

2. The volcanic basalt.

The Dirt

The most photogenic of the volcanic soils are those with the *picon*—the black ash that squeaks like black snow—found on Lanzarote and La Palma. On Lanzarote, the vines are planted dramatically in huge round nests, burrowed into pits in the ash to protect them from the strong African winds. On La Palma, the vines in the south are planted on the sides of volcanos, even when old vines seem spindly in the poor soils.

But Tenerife is the largest of all the islands and, even though there's no *picon*, it's where most of the action is happening. Called the Land of Eternal Spring, Tenerife has the most varied climate and soils of the seven islands. Its dominating feature is one huge volcano, El Teide, the world's third-tallest island volcano. On its north side, you feel as though you're in the wet and windy Loire region; while on the south side, it is as sunny and dry as if you're in the south of France. For a few miles, toward the top of El Teide, you can see how the once violent volcano created a never-ending moon landscape of hardened, jagged lava that looks like it will take another million years to weather into proper vineyard soils.

Today, we see a region trying to become relevant. There has been pressure to modernize and to plant varieties like Cabernet and Merlot, but to follow that road would be foolish and disrespectful to the old vines of grapes more suited to the area. The man that will take the island to international acclaim is a visionary named Roberto Santana. Born in Tenerife, with basalt in his blood, he gathered a group of friends from wine school and started a wine company called Envínate. They make wine throughout Spain, pinpointing lands that can express "Atlantic" characters. One of his first sites was the abandoned vineyard on the cliffs of Taganana, a tiny village located half an hour north-east of Santa Cruz, the biggest city on the island.

In this place, there is iron-rich soil and black rocks, left over from lava flows. Thankfully, it's been a long time since El Teide blew its top. Hopefully Santana can continue bringing back the field blend of the vineyard, from the almost wild vines and soil that turn the wines into liquid iron, for a long time.

The Grapes

Most Canary Island grapes—the good ones—also grow all over Spain. For whites, the most prominent is Listán Blanco, also known as Palomino, the grape of sherry. It is a relatively thin-skinned and low in acid, which makes for a quicker-drinking and pleasant white wine. It is for sure in Roberto's parcel in Santa Cruz, and it blends well with a myriad of other grapes. It often tastes like a direct translation of the rugged sea air. Listán Negro is the primary red grape of the region, and doesn't show up much elsewhere in the world. Herbal-tasting Negramoll came to the Canaries from southwestern Spain. Malvasia is planted all over the Mediterranean, and it is famed for making sweet wine. The grape once had an exalted reputation in La Palma. Over the decades, it has been sacrificed, ripped out to plant banana plantations instead.

- Envínate, Táganan; Tenerife (organic)
- Dolores Cabrera, La Arancaria; Tenerife (organic)
- Borja Perez, Ignois; Tenerife (organic)
- Envínate, Benje; Tenerife (organic)
- Frontón de Oro; Gran Canaria (organic)

The Willamette Valley

Ah, so you love Oregon Pinot Noir? You like it better than California—less thick, less candied—but can't figure out why? Could it possibly be the place? The climate? The attitude? The soils?

As it turns out, it's all of the above.

The Dirt

Oregon's Willamette Valley is a 150 mile-long stretch from just above Portland down south, stopping just around Eugene. This is where the Pinot action in Oregon takes place. The climate is wet, with about 40 inches of rain a year. The growing season is long yet unpredictable. Great stretches of hot and dry summer days are often thrown into the mix. Spend any time there talking to winemakers and you'll hear the term Jory. That's their soil: colluvial sediments, a mixture of rock and fine sand sediments from cliffs and hills, plus a bunch of stuff thrown about by the great Missoula floods, commingled with the main event, 15-million-year-old, deeply weathered basalt. Fly into PDX and you'll see the volcanoes, Mount Hood and Mount Jefferson, out of the plane window. They are still considered active, but most of the volcanic soils came from the time before man, when this whole area was covered in water. Given all of that rain and sun, there's a lot of degradation, and the red soils of Jory are iron-rich and sandy mixed with clay. If I had written this book six years ago I might have excluded Oregon, because there were few makers that worked naturally and made wines I found exciting. On top of that, in one of the wettest growing areas in America, they tend to unnecessarily abuse the soil with irrigation. Why? I am forever dumbfounded. But more and more, there are those who are dry farming, meaning ditching the use of irrigation pipes. There are also more people working naturally. Today, I find Oregon one of the most exciting spots for interesting winemaking in this country, and much of it is on those hills of the Willamette Valley.

One of the original standouts in the valley is Eyrie Vineyards, created by the founding father of Oregon wine country, David Lett. His winery, now run by his thoughtful son Jason, is still at the top of the heap. Jason is one of the best generational succession stories ever. I believe he and his father set the stage for the newcomers, even if they don't know it. Jason is intimately familiar with the land's history, noting that "volcanic eruptions ladled out this soupy lava. It flowed across and over the top of continental shelf material and sediments. It created this layer cake of continental shelf basalt, marine sediment, and on top of that, more soupy lava. You can see the layers in the soil, there are bookmarks in the way the colors change if you take a cross-section of soils. Each of these flows has a different chemical and physical composition."

There are very few examples of Pinot Noir on basalt other than in the land between the Rhône and the Loire, the Auvergne, where, like Oregon, the wines tend more to layers of savory. I asked Jason if his dad had any angst about planting Pinot Noir on soil that was dramatically different than limestone, considered the golden rule for that grape.

"No angst," he said. "Dad's whole thing, he didn't care about the chemical—he was more concerned with climate. He looked at some of the marine sedimentary soils, but those were sand and shales . . . and unpredictable, water-wise. He wanted more predictable . . . he wanted to grow without irrigation, and Jory really excels for that. Not all basalts are created equal." The key, Jason says, lies in the variation in the kind of clay that binds the soil together, "There's a kind that swells when wet. You don't want that! It shrinks and cracks in dry weather and does not aerate." His dad realized that the clay in the Jory soils was kaolin, the kind that removes impurities from the skin and is often used in makeup. Unlike what some of the literature says, Lett believed that it is good for the vines. "Instead of blowing up like a balloon, [the clay] swells in two directions in a series of flat sheets, like planes of glass. That's why it's possible to walk in the wet vineyard without slipping on your butt. Also, when summers are dry, the microscopic bits of clay retain moisture."

When David Lett was looking at climate, he was looking for a match for Pinot Noir. The Willamette weather is not that unlike Burgundy, though it has warmer winters and hotter summers. The second major consideration was the presence of slopes and hillsides. Only after those two factors were met did he narrow in on the soil. And what he needed was a soil that played well with the delicate Pinot vine. "How water relates to the plant is super important. If you irrigate it and chemical-ize it, you can lose it all by dislodging the vitality. The plant needs the whole community." Mineral exchange is vastly different in basic soils like limestone versus the acidic soils of basalt. In the end, Jason says, when it comes to wine, "You're tasting a collaboration."

The Grapes

Oregon in general is known for Pinot Noir, but only in the Willamette Valley is it a given. With the proper intervention, you can make a California-style, big Pinot in Oregon, but for the most part the wines here have more savoriness and less solar-powered fruit. A number of other grapes do well here. Gamay will have a future. In the south, you're going to get a bunch of experiments from Syrah to Tempranillo. It's hotter down there and the soil is different, so from Applegate vineyards, expect a sunnier wine. White grapes are abundant. Chardonnay? Sure. Eyrie's is great and well-mannered. Melon de Bourgogne, the one which makes

Muscadet and is usually found in the Loire Valley, is coming in strong in Oregon where it shows more fruit than its Loire sister. Riesling does very well here, though with by no means the sophistication of the slopes and schist of the Mosel. The Columbia Gorge, an hour's ride from Portland, is showing some extremely interesting wines. I would give almost anything from there a chance. They are growing some impressive Pinot Noir, Pinot Gris, and, from what I hear, some damned interesting Mencía.

WHO TO DRINK

- Eyrie Vineyards (organic)
- Bow & Arrow (organic, biodynamic)
- Montinore (biodynamic)
- Montebruno (organic, biodynamic)
- Day Wines (organic, biodynamic)
- J.K. Carriere (organic, biodynamic)
- Minimus Wines (organic, biodynamic)
- Beckham Estate (organic, biodynamic)
- Cameron Winery (organic)
- Swick Wines (organic)
- Evening Land (biodynamic)

TUFF

Somewhere in between basalt and granite is another form of igneous rock that comes from fire: tuff. Because of its name, tuff is often confused with the limestone tuffeau (see the Touraine section on page 148 for more on that). However, it couldn't be more different. Tuff is an extrusive, blasted, fragmented lava rock, an amalgam of stuff from the volcano blast and silica-rich rhyolite, which ranges from a porous gray to a smooth, shiny glass. It shows up in Tuscany but there's another very eccentric, exciting, and tuff-rich region worth talking about.

Alto Piemonte

Long before I had any idea what volcanic soil was, I knew I was attracted to the wines of the Alto Piemonte. They grew a favorite of mine, Nebbiolo, even though they often called it a different name. The most important quality though was that the wines spoke of a place.

The Alto Piemonte, so close to the lake district, about an hour from the Milan airport, is the highest elevation zone in Piemonte, about 1,480 feet up. Once you get past the fashion outlets like Loro Piana, which have absorbed the dwindling vineyards, and into the vines, the air is bracing and there's an element of starkness about it all.

This part of the world has a clutch of tiny DOCs few care about, which is ludicrous. Among them are some beauties: Carema, Lessona, Fara, Ghemme, Sizzano, and a trio that's the most well-known, Gattinara, Boca, and Bramaterra. There are two DOCGs, Ghemme and Gattinara. Red wine is chiefly made made from Spanna, the local name for Nebbiolo, responsible for the glorious Barolos in Piemonte. There are a few other supporting varieties; I've never seen a white from the area.

The wines have this snappy, crunchy Alpine character, which means for the most part herbal notes and freshness come first in the taste profile. While in some years, some of the regions, like Lessona, can get jammy, for the most part the wines have bony, not hedonistic, qualities. These are more like a good book, chock-full of ideas and thoughts, that makes you come back. The two regions I'm most drawn to are Boca and Bramaterra.

The Dirt

The soils of both Boca and Bramaterra are derived from a mix of intrusive porphyry and extrusive igneous rock, lava, or tuff. The tuff, as mentioned before, is rich in silica and iron and contains larger crystals of quartz in a fine-grained matrix.

The geological mystery here is something they call Valsesia, the supervolcano. Valsesia was active 280 million years ago, and was only revealed when the African and European plates collided. After about 10 million years of eruptions, an even more surprising disaster happened: The volcano imploded. This created not only an enormous caldera, but three lakes as well: Orta, Maggiore, and Varese.

Now imagine what the hell would happen if El Teide or Mount Etna collapsed in on itself. Boca was once perched on the tip of a volcano, but one would never know it from standing in the vines that grow on its remnants. In fact, when I visited one of my favorite producers from there, Vallana, I had no idea of its explosive history.

I used to drink gallons of Vallana Spanna when I was in my late twenties, and decades later, I finally got to go to the source. I asked the winemaker Francis Fogarty (in charge of the family domain along with his sister Marina) to drive me into the tiny 22-acre DOC. Boca occupies the highest elevation in the area. As we approached his land, all around me I saw odd-looking Maggiorina trellising. This is a sort of *albarello*, but they are not free-form. Instead, the vines are pulled upward in four directions, like tentacles hanging out to dry. It's a system that was developed in the 1700s and is quite rare, as it requires a lot of work. But on that visit to Vallana, there were no vines; they'd been grubbed up, awaiting replanting. We arrived at a naked plot, isolated on an incline overlooking the huge monastery nearby. "See the different-colored soils?" Fogarty asked, pointing to veins of rose, red, and white dirt. He explained that the highly acidic porphyry soils, which are typically located a few kilometers underground, might be why the wines have an even longer life than the wines of Barolo, where the grapes grow on sediments. The soil in Boca out-acids those of nearby Ghemme and Gattinara, perhaps the reason the DOC rules require the addition of other approved grapes to soften up the wine and add gentle aromatics.

Another characteristic of the native soil, Fogarty explains, is that "because the mother rock is so close to the soil, the roots actually manage to grow inside the little gaps in the rocks and almost fuse with the rock." He thinks this anchoring of the vines helps to prevent erosion and develops better fruit. On top of this, Boca has a very complicated geomorphology, which provides for a very rich collection of microclimates in a comparatively small area. In Boca, farmers have to deal with great variation in soil and microclimate conditions.

Over on the other side of the Sesia River is the DOC Bramaterra. This is another tiny DOC, just 52 acres, (though still about three times bigger than Boca). There are plenty of differences between the two. Here, they call the grape Nebbiolo instead of Spanna. Both Bramaterra and Boca have porphyry soils, but in Bramaterra's soil one can find the rock they call *porfido tufaceo*, which contains elements like silicon and boron—also found in the pumice of Etna—but partnered with a significant bed of limestone, which gives it a bit of a twist. Underground aquifers give the plant needed water during the driest seasons. But like Boca, the problem here is too much rain, not too little. I met two of the DOC's finest growers, Antoniotti and Mattia Odilio, and tasted their 2014s, which I thought were stunning—and even more surprising because it was a monsoon year in Italy (and in most of Europe). Because of the rain there was a lot of disease, such as mildew, and difficulty ripening the grapes—and when they ripened there was mold. It just goes to show that a bad vintage usually simply indicates how much work there was to do in the vineyard. If you do the work as the Odilios do, the wines can still be stellar.

The Odilios explained that there is some limestone and clay in the region, but mostly it is grounded in porphyry, as in Boca. But in both Bramaterra and Boca, the porphyry is right at the top due to the ancient supervolcano eruption and is acidic and rich in iron. Both regions are capable of beauty and yes, both regions are being pushed out by the fashion industry, the vineyards being replaced by outlet stores. It's depressing. How can a region capable of giving such gifts to the world be abandoned? If you're lucky, you'll get to drink a Bramaterra wine and then go and compare it to a southern one using the same grapes, Nebbiolo, but raised in different soils, different climates, though just an hour's journey separates the two.

Between the two large lakes, Orta and Maggiore, the weather-blocking capacity of the Alpine mountains protects Alto Piemonte from extremes. The winters are cold and dry. Spring brings mild temperatures and rain. Summers are hot, and it stays that way through September. Then, during the October harvest—though this may change in the present warming global climate—the weather dips into cool nights.

The Grapes

This is Nebbiolo country, the same grape that gives you Barolo and Barbaresco. Here, however, the local name is Spanna. Both Boca and Bramaterra also boast vines of Croatina, Vespolina, and Uva Rara. Vespolina is a sibling of Nebbiolo, and it's a delicate creature, prone to rot. It fell out of favor in the 19th century after a louse with the name of phylloxera destroyed most of the vines of Europe. The cure turned out to be planting vines on American rootstock. However, there was a cost. Its taste. Famed British wine critic, Jancis Robinson, writes in her book *Wine Grapes*, that it failed to ripen well on its new "feet," as rootstock is sometimes called. And so a wine which originally gave so much sugar it attracted wasps is now somewhat subdued and is used in blends. Uva Rara is a very old grape in the area and it brings a perfume to the mix. Croatina (called Bonarda in the Oltrepò Pavese DOC) is the last piece of the puzzle. This grape might find its way into a 100 percent version (called a single varietal), but is generally best when added into the mix.

- Vallana; Boca (sustainable and organic)
- Antoniotti Odilio; Bramaterra (organic)
- Colombera & Garella; Lessona and Bramaterra (organic)

GRANITE

Granite may be a common material for countertops and sidewalks, but don't slip into the pitfall of thinking it's common. The rock is everywhere, sure. It appears in the Earth's basement, mezzanine, and top floor; most of the Earth's surface and mountain ranges. An intrusive igneous rock, granite started its life in molten form, cooling slowly under pressure and commingling with glowing quartzes. When granite weathers over millions of years, it produces a range of soils: mica, quartz, loess, and clay, all of which easily crumble into mixtures of gravel, sand, and silt-sized particles.

What makes granite one of the world's greatest soils for grapes? Granite is associated with an edgy structure and a needle-like tang of acidity and freshness. This is often referred to as "minerality." Terroir consultant Pedro Parra, the Chilean geologist and winemaker, believes that with granite soil, the magic comes across in the tannins. The resulting wine is always a little drier and the sensation of raspiness is felt more in the back of the mouth, almost in the jawbone, often with a nervous, high-pitched sensation.

Wines from granite frequently have subdued aromatics when young but blossom with age. In the Muscadet, the wines can hint at tastes and smells of wet cardboard, which can mimic a corked wine. But after couple of years, like a caterpillar turned butterfly, the wine has tremendous majesty

What special physical qualities does granite-derived soil have? For starters, the degraded rock is low in pH, meaning the soil is acidic. The degradation, according to geologist Kevin Pogue, allows important metals such as iron to be delivered to the plant's system, but yet, being so stony and acidic, the soil is usually low on nutrition. The low fertility of granite soils, most often with its low clay content, ensures that a plant won't yield a lot of fruit. Lower yields are considered a necessity for a higher quality of wine. Also, with the right amount of weathering, granitic soil drains well. In wet years, that means that the vines won't sit in their own muck and take in too much water, and the roots won't dig down deep.

Coincidence or not, some of my favorite wine regions have granite soils. In France alone, this includes important chunks of the Beaujolais, Muscadet, and northern Rhône. I started to ponder the grapes that thrived in that particular soil. There was Gamay, Syrah, and Melon. What linked these wines was a certain freshness, a savoriness, structure, and importantly, more subdued fruit flavors and aromas. There are some who believe in the supremacy of grapes grown on limestone, as in Burgundy, but I'd put granite-grown grapes right up there with the best.

I asked Parra to give me his thoughts on the intrusive volcanic rock. Parra has an outsized passion for terroir. Rocks are his best friends, yet I was not quite prepared for his emotional response: "After limestone, granite is my favorite soil type." Then he waxed almost mystical: "Granite means that there is lots of quartz. Quartz means energy, but more importantly, quartz means porosity. Porosity equals air. With the roots, water movement equals life. This is all very simple, but you don't get this combination in soil very often. You see, granite creates very healthy and deep roots." This interplay is the reason healthy soil, teeming with beneficial bacteria and funghi, is essential to the notion of place.

The Northern Rhône

I always took granite for granted. Then, one summer when I was driving south from Burgundy, about 40 minutes from the village of Vienne on the A7, I was in the middle of singing "Boots of Spanish Leather" along with Bob Dylan when I looked up. "Wow," I said, as I left the lush sedimentary limestone of southern Burgundy and entered the igneous granitic austerity of the northern Rhône. Seeing the gradual transformation was startling.

The northern Rhône is known for its granitic soils, steep slopes, crazy-strong winds, taut acid-driven apricots, and the world's best Syrah. On that particular trip, I was on the A7, but my favorite way to go is on the little truck route that winds down from the north not far from Lyon, through the charming little villages towards Tournon-sur-Rhône. It's the best way to understand where they are. The first vineyard you reach is the famed Côte-Rôtie (where they have more metamorphic rocks like gneiss and mica-schist than granite), and then the AOC *monopole* Condrieu, the little village known solely for its white wine from the floral Viognier grape. At times, with the steep rolling hills and the rurality, you could almost think you're in Vermont, except there's the Rhône River to the east, and apricots everywhere instead of apples.

In comparison to the southern Rhône, famed for its rich wines made from Grenache, the northern region is considered a cooler climate. While the summers can be roasting hot, they can get more rainfall. Winters, however, can be punishing, especially with the impossible wind. And that was what I experienced when I was standing with Hervé Souhaut in his Saint-Joseph vineyard and my cheeks were getting whipped by the January gusts. Under my boots, the iced-over soil teemed with cacti, a reminder of the summer's heat. Everything was matted and beaten down by the winds, the Bise and the Mistral, supposedly at their worst in the northern Rhône in March and April. In January, though, it was already brutal. Hervé bent down and picked up what seemed to be a compressed rock. It was pinkish red and laced with iron. As he pressed the flat rock into my palm, he identified it: *arzelle*, a crumbly type of granite. I cracked off a piece. The stone crumbled as if it were a sheet of brittle paper. I thought of the granite I had seen in other places, like New Hampshire or the Sierra foothills, but what Hervé had handed me was totally unfamiliar. Still, it shared the same heritage as its harder cousins, formed under immense heat and pressure far below the Earth's surface.

The Dirt

Those early days of geology were dramatic. It was a violent clash between the tectonic plates that lay under the Massif Central, the central part of France, and the younger mountains, the Alps, which caused the Rhône Valley. This giant collision occurred about 45 million years ago and created a rift that allowed the Mediterranean Ocean to flood the valley in the south. When the waters finally dried up, the resulting decomposition of marine life left a belt of limestone in the southern Rhône. Meanwhile, the violent volcanic activity in the Massif Central about 300 million years ago had already laid the groundwork for the northern Rhône regions. The roiling molten blood of the Earth remained under pressure and, over millions of years, slowly degraded and mixed with its other elements to create granite.

When decomposed, granite soil can be quite sandy. Without a lot of clay, as on the slopes of the northern Rhône, the soils have poor water retention. Rain drains through it like water through a tea strainer. In wet regions and years, this can be terrific, and I've had some fabulous wines from the northern Rhône in flood years. Dry seasons are way more difficult. The vines suffer more, since the soils can't hold on to the water. When the vines go thirsty, that affects the thickness of the grape skins, the tannins, and the fruit flavors. However, Syrah is not as greedy for water as other grapes, so it can survive the area's frequently dry summers. Because of this dryness, the region is also prone to erosion. With the growing number of organic wine grapes that are farmed without using chemicals, the soils are more vibrant and anchored with beneficial plants, and so the erosion issue is less severe. And when the wine is made, somehow, the magic of that Syrah grape matched to that granitic soil mixes subtly in the bottle.

"The match between Syrah and granite is a perfect one," Parra says. "We call a grape like Syrah 'elastic'" (meaning so juicy that even if you try to make a bad wine, you really can't). "Granite gives the sweet, juicy fruit a mineral side." He added that without this mineral side, you only have a "happy wine," by which he means a wine that is just sunshine and fruit; ultimately tasty, but not attention-getting.

You see, the best grape and soil combos mean that you don't have to farm heroically to make it work. It's the same as in any love match. Chemistry, along with ease, usually means a long life for any couple.

Hermitage-based Jean-Louis Chave is local royalty. He gave a fabulous interview to Levi Dalton, the host of the podcast *I'll Drink to That*, on the character of the soils in his region, in which he stated flat-out that "limestone and granite are each other's opposite." He said that in a dry year, the top part of his soil suffers from drought, but down below, the clay keeps the humidity, which of course is the glory of clay. The granite, he says, can give the reds some aggressive tannins. The white grapes—the Roussanne and Marsanne—gain finesse. Chave also noted that while the Crozes-Hermitage DOC gets a bad rap (because there's quite a bit of clay in the soil and that can make a flabbier wine), the hill of Hermitage, which is on the same eastern side of the Rhône as Crozes, is exalted. Chave talked about the way his vines behaved in the Les Bessards vineyard, the one in his portfolio with the most profound and intense granite: "It is all completely crushed rocks. The vines get green, dark leaves." It is said that the grapes from there are extremely tannic. Meanwhile, in the Le Méal vineyard, the grapes are said to be richer and riper. The reason behind this, Chave said, is that "the soils there have a higher pH. There's small pebbles and the leaves are a more pale yellow green." The leaves have their distinct color because the intake of iron is more difficult in a higher pH soil.

It was validating to hear one of the most respected voices of the area say that you cannot talk about terroir without being at least organic. "You want the roots to go down deep enough to express the soil," Chave says. "Being organic is important for the natural yeast; they might be the same in all vineyards, but the proportion is different [in different soils]. On clay, the vines have more power. On the poor soils of granite they struggle all the time. As long as the roots go down to the cracks of the granite, the vines will live forever. They will build around and change the structure of the soil, and make more soil. Even in the drought, they will do well. Grand terroir is where the vine is naturally balanced."

Winemaking in the Northern Rhône

Sometimes there's nothing to discuss in the way a region makes and grows their wine. But with others, such as the northern Rhône, it's essential to know what makes the area tick and what makes the difference.

Here, vines are most usually attached to stakes (called *échalas*), just like tomato plants. This works well on steep slopes for optimum grape ripeness while maximizing the amount of vines one can plant.

The grapes are picked just before they achieve sweetness, so all elements are in balance and not too focused on the fruit flavor.

Then there are forms of fermentation to choose from. Many modern-style winemakers—in search for what they think is a cleaner, fruit-driven style—destem the grapes, vinify in stainless steel, and sometimes move the wine to age into newer barrels. But my favorite winemakers seem to prefer the traditional method of using the whole cluster, that allows for a spiciness and deeper complexity. They throw the full, intact grape cluster into either open-top concrete or wooden vats and do a little stomping to get the juice to start flowing. Then, after the wine is finished, it goes into an old barrel to age until the winemaker deems it to be ready, usually about one and a half years after its vintage date.

The Grapes

When one grape gets popular in a region, all others seem to disappear, and that was the case with the northern Rhône. If you're lucky enough to get some Gamay (See Beaujolais, page 94), you'll be in for a treat. There's barely any left in town, but it's an animalistic and muscular fruit. For whites, up in Condrieu, right next to Côte-Rôtie, it is all about the honeysuckle-like Viognier grape. Great whites also come from Marsanne and Roussanne, often showing up down south. But to talk about the north is to talk about Syrah.

In her book *Wine Grapes*, Jancis Robinson punched holes in the theory that the somewhat tannic Syrah grape came from the Persian city of Shiraz. While it's a poetic idea, the fruit's name most likely evolved from its oldest clone, Serine. The name's root means "late ripening," which describes Syrah accurately.

Genetically speaking, Syrah's great-grandfather is Pinot. But its parents are more local. Mondeuse Blanche, Syrah's mother, originates in the nearby Savoie region of France. Around the corner is Ardèche, where Syrah's dad, Dureza, was born. This means that Syrah is a total northern Rhône homegirl. That might be why nowhere else in the world can bring out such a deep expression of its characteristics. Syrah's taste varies depending on where it's grown, on what soil and in which climate, and what decisions are made in the winemaking and picking processes. But as far as classic flavors go, they are: olive, bacon, meat, blood, herbs, laurel, rosemary, and earth.

Until the 20th century, the Syrah grape wasn't grown elsewhere outside of the Rhône except for Australia. Today, Syrah thrives outside of France. It pops up in Tuscany, Chile, and South Africa. It is prevalent as Shiraz in Australia (where some of the oldest vines in the Barossa Valley, dating back to 1843, still exist). California has been trying to make it click.

California, though, has a Syrah problem. Winemakers love it, but it hasn't sold well. It's hard to tell what the exact problem is. Sometimes I believe that the issue is with producers who claim to be inspired by the great winemakers of Cornas, but then turn around and make fruit bombs. These Syrah-based, Napa Cabernet look-alikes bear no resemblance to the real thing, so it's no surprise they get rejected.

But it's not hopeless! Today, there are winemakers hard at work trying to interpret the grape to suit its new homes. Some are picking early to make wines with lower alcohol. But this isn't a perfect solution, as often that just means that the resulting wines are merely under-wined. So what's the answer? There's a great winemaking team in Sonoma, Arnot-Roberts, consisting of Duncan Arnot Meyers and Nathan Lee Roberts, two childhood friends who grew up to make serious wine together. They found a spot in foggy Marin County where the grapes struggle to ripen. This is exciting, as many theorize that the best grapes come from where they struggle the most. Arnot-Roberts grapes are picked well into

November (when normal picking times can be September). While their Clary Ranch Syrah does get that black olive taste of the Rhône, there's something else, as if the grape were doing an interpretive dance using the elements of fog and loam instead of wind and granite.

Steve Edmunds, meanwhile, makes a wine under the label Edmunds St. John. He has been working at it since the late '80s. Though he doesn't source from organic grapes, he is a trailblazer of restrained Syrah in California. Through the years he has never strayed from his vision, no matter what fashion trends come and go. The vines he uses are grown on both loam (clay and sand) and granite. He finds the wines he makes from granite edgier. Some of the vineyards he works with are up in the Sierra Nevada foothills in the decomposed granite territory where another fine winemaker, Hank Beckmeyer of La Clarine Farm, works and lives. His terroir is 2,600 feet up on a flattish ridge, its dry, dusty territory a home for rattlesnakes and tumbleweed and wild sage. For some reason, on his land, his Syrah, and the one from down the road, develops a tart, luscious pomegranate-like flavor. And maybe it's the power of suggestion, but I swear I can feel his rugged site filled with wild sage when I taste his Syrahs.

Some say that Australia, like California, where much of the vine is planted on flat land, produces wines that only reflect the sun. Places like the northern Rhône, where the vine is mostly planted on the slopes, are said to reflect the soil. Sun for photosynthesis is essential, but when coupled with certain farming methods and picking at ultra-ripeness, the results can be sloppy and syrupy—exactly what Shiraz's reputation has devolved into.

But even in Australia, the wine is growing up. In the southeast, outside of Melbourne in the district of Victoria, there is a granite belt where ex-filmmaker Julian Castagna makes wine on his estate, the Castagna Vineyard, located outside of Beechworth. He calls his Shiraz "Syrah" and works his land according to the traditions of the northern

Rhône. He works his fermentation in similar ways to the northern Rhône as well, in open-top fermenters, and throws the grapes into them on their full bunches. The results are terrific. All in all, he tries to work with the grape so as to not overemphasize the heat and the sun. As a result, the Castagna wines manage to pare back the granite and show a particularly Australian expression of the grape in the soil, avoiding the pitfalls of may other full and fat Syrahs.

Now, I'm not suggesting that the northern Rhône is the only place to grow the vine, or that the grape should be restricted to living in decomposed granite. Obviously, the Côte-Rôtie of Jean-Michel Stephan or Stéphane Otheguy show that the vine works beautifully in metamorphic soils of mica-schist and gneiss. Yet, there is something fabulous about the granite. I love the way it keeps the fruit in check and also helps to sand down the tannins and give structure. Yes, there are fewer viruses on granite. All of that is true. What I am proposing is that Syrah on granite in the northern Rhône should be the reference point for all other winemakers. One must learn why it works there and respect the knowledge, just as one must learn the basics of language or music before one can excel at improvisation.

When navigating wines from the Rhône, it's important to understand the appellations. For red wines, on the left bank there's Crozes-Hermitage and Hermitage; on the right bank, there's Cornas, Côte-Rôtie, and Saint-Joseph. While most famous for reds, there are some whites—and three zones that only make whites. Saint-Péray, on limestone, is a little-known area in the south that makes white and sparkling wine of Marsanne and Roussanne grapes. The others are on granite. Condrieu, just south of Côte-Rôtie, is devoted to the floral grape, Viognier. So too is the Château-Grillet, another all-white zone with 3.8-hectare vineyard that's a *monopole* (one sole owner owns the entire appellation). And as far as the red appellations? All but Côte-Rôtie and Cornas, like Saint-Péray, make some white wine from Marsanne and Roussanne.

CROZES-HERMITAGE: Gaining appellation status in 1937, this wine region is right near Tain-l'Hermitage (and the Valrhona chocolate factory), and yet has had a hard time getting respect. Why? In 1958, the AOC expanded the region greatly. That was almost corrected in 1989, when the acreage was decreased to about 3,000 acres, but the region still has the most land under vines. Too much of the land in the appellation isn't great, however, and there's plenty of vine planted on poor-quality flat land, where the apricot trees used to grow. This will be your cheapest-priced bottle for the area, but like everything else, it's getting more expensive all the time. The best vineyards are those northeast parcels where the hillsides are relatively steep and full of granite soils: Les Chassis, Les Sept Chemins, and Les Meysonniers.

HERMITAGE: Hermitage also landed its AOC designation in 1937. It's made up of one large parcel. The southwest side of a mostly granitic hill, it's topped with a Hollywood-like sign that reads "Hermitage." Its finest vineyards are Les Bessards, Le Méal, l'Ermite, Peleat, and Les Beaumes. The wines are classy and expensive. It is also famed for a small amount of sweet white wine called Vin de Paille, named for the practice where the grapes are left on straw mats to dry.

CORNAS: This is the smallest of the northern Rhône appellations and one of my favorites. The appellation became 'legal' right after Hermitage, in 1938. Just walking in the vines—set into its amphitheater-like bowl, is inspirational. It's also packed with some really great winemakers. The soil is mostly finely decomposed granite, terribly steep and with a sprinkling here and there of limestone. The warmest of the appellations, it's dry and parched and sheltered in many spots from the fierce Mistral wind. This appellation's rules require the wines to be 100 percent Syrah. Also, for some reason, there's a long legacy of the wines here being "rustic." Absolutely forget that ancient history. The most famous vineyards here are Reynard, which is mostly granite, and Les Chaillots, which has some limestone, depending on where you are.

SAINT-JOSEPH: This joined the AOC club in 1956. Named after Saint Joseph—who presided over scorned husbands—this glorious vineyard region is 37 miles long, almost the size of the Côte d'Or. That distance covers a lot of ups and downs, and the region has suffered from a stupid expansion allowing some questionable land to be planted. But when it works, to my palate, these Syrah can be among the silkiest, sexiest wines out there. It was originally known as Vin de Mauves (after Mauves, the main town dedicated to Saint Joseph) and was mentioned in Victor Hugo's *Les Misérables*. This area's wine was supposedly favored by Louis XII (ruled 1498–1515), who owned a vineyard known as Clos de Tournon. In 1979, the appellation was allowed to include up to 10 percent of the white grapes Marsanne and Roussanne. The most famous of its vineyards are Sainte-Épine and Cessieux.

CÔTE-RÔTIE: The direct translation of this hill is "roasted (rôtie) slope (côte)." With ancient Roman roots, this historically glorious region was established as an AOC in 1940 but almost disappeared after WWII. At the time, it had maybe only 130 acres planted; with such a small production, they couldn't sell their wines. Since that time, it has been transformed with a nice little spike in sales in the '80s and a zoom to fame in the '90s. As a result, the wines almost disappeared again, but not from lack of sales. Instead, the problem was a lack of authenticity, with new kinds of wood and modern technology being used that resulted in a vintage that strayed from the traditional profile.

There is a tiny handful of wines holding up the area's lapsed reputation. But then this region isn't known for a whole lot of granite; it's mostly gneiss and schist. However, there are two famed hills here worth noting: Côte Blonde is mostly granite and metamorphic gneiss, while Côte Brune is mostly a mica-rich, heavy schist, referred to as micha schist. The rules allow up to 20 percent Viognier in the fermentation. If you ever come across the wines from the producer Gentaz-Dervieux, treat the discovery as you would a miracle; no longer made, these wines are legendary.

Winemaker Profile: Hirotake Ooka of Domaine de la Grande Colline.

How did a nice Japanese boy like Hirotake Ooka get to Cornas—a secluded, almost xenophobic place with steep hills and hard-working vignerons—that's about as far away in aesthetic as you can get from Tokyo? In Japanese, "oh" means big and "*oka*" means hill, so it's tempting to think there was some karma going on—winemaking was his fate.

In 1997, Ooka left his Japanese home for Bordeaux to learn winemaking. The impetus for change was a bottle from the Cornas master Thierry Allemand, a winemaker who made his mark by creating some stunning wines made without the preservative sulfur added. He has made his mark on almost everyone who has made Syrah in the world.

Having sniffed that truth of wine, Ooka headed to the northern Rhône in search of work with the master himself. Rebuffed, he landed a vineyard management job with Guigal—not exactly a bastion of the natural wine world, but at least he was in the right neighborhood. In time, Allemand relented and there, in the hills of Cornas, Ooka worked. He made his first wines under his own Le Canon label in 2001. In 2002, 19 virgin hectares in Cornas came up for sale. It was within sight of Allemand's vineyard and winery on the splice between Saint-Péray and Cornas. This opportunity preceded the region's huge uptick in prices (which could now run more than a million dollars for two acres for cultivated land). Besides, the soil was chemical-free. This was the beginning of Ooka's Domaine de la Grande Colline, which of course means "big hill."

I was late when I drove into Ooka's driveway off the main drag in Saint-Péray. As I got out of the car into his yard, in front of a colorful vegetable garden, I had to wonder what Franck Balthazar, the vigneron I had just visited, meant when he snickered, "Ask Hirotake about his 2013 vintage!"

Ooka was waiting for me, and I was utterly charmed by the bevy of small naked children running around the house while fresh sushi perfumed the air with umami. That was certainly an interesting image to have in mind as we drove a short distance to his wine cave, over which hung an almost obscured sign: "Caveau de Crussol."

Inside, we shivered next to the stone, which was weeping with the cold and humidity. All bottles and crevices were clad in darkened furballs of mold.

"Never above 11 degrees," Hirotake said. (That's 52 degrees Farenheit.)

The cold helps with natural winemaking, the kind of winemaking that starts with organic viticulture and has none of the many approved legal additives, except for perhaps a minute bit of sulfur dioxide. It is the kind of wine that Ooka believes that he's mastered, at least for the reds. He said this with such humility in his voice that it didn't seem like bragging. His reds, for the most part, are vinified using whole bunches of grapes, stems and all. The grapes start to ferment from the inside—as if fermenting carbonically (enzymatic fermentation)—but then are quickly transferred into what is known as alcoholic fermentation, where the fruit is crushed and the yeasts start to eat the sugar, resulting in alcohol. The wine stays in barrels until it is ready to bottle.

Part of Ooka's practice is to never move a wine until it's stable. For example, his 2011 Saint-Joseph had 36 months of *élevage*, which is the term used for the aging of the wine before bottling. The exception, however, is his bread and butter wine, the less expensive (though delicious) Le Canon, released as a relatively fresh wine. He also makes a nouveau-like bottling for the Japanese. All are under synthetic cork. "That way, if there is something wrong, it is my fault. Not something out of my control."

Dinner called to him, but I begged to see his land. He agreed, and we headed back into the hills, and turned through a neighbor's backyard, to vines hiding in the shadow of Allemand's *cuverie*. Ooka only farms 3.5 hectares out of all his land, which is divided into twelve different parcels. The one we walked out to see was a ridiculously steep vineyard, far steeper than anything I had seen before in Cornas. Ooka's name now made complete sense.

The vines stood in a romp of weeds and plants and vines planted to high density, at about 8,000 plants per hectare. The air was crackling and fragrant. The surrounding aroma from the *garrigue*, the mixture of wild herbs that freely grew all around us, was wafting up after the recent spot of rain. "So," I finally asked, "what did happen in 2013?"

It turns out that he wanted to follow an extreme version of Masanobu Fukuoka's methods. Fukuoka was the Japanese philosopher-farmer who wrote the poetic and influential farming book *One-Straw Revolution*, on what is often called "do-nothing farming." That term is something of a misnomer but it's very much an observational approach to farming that uses no chemicals and depends on plants to move and aerate the earth instead of plowing. Ooka chose not to treat the soil, trusting instead that the natural environment would be all the protection he needed. However, nature wasn't kind. In 2013 he lost everything to rot. It was devastating, but he didn't seem perturbed. "I was prepared for the risk," he said. And now he has learned. He will spray when he needs to.

"And what are your thoughts about how granite works with the Syrah plants here?" I asked him.

He told me how there was very little soil and very little clay, so there were not many nutritive elements and very little water. "In addition, our vines are on slopes that accentuate this phenomenon. This creates a very difficult life condition for vines [and] leads to a very immoderate vigor, which results in a small crop," he said.

When I asked him about the effect on the wine's taste, he had this to offer: "For example, between the Reynard and Chaillots vineyards," he said, naming two of the most famous vineyards of Cornas, the Chaillots has granite terroir, but there is also limestone and more clay. On the clay, the wine shows a power with massive and smoky aromas. Reynard, however, is a terroir of pure granite, which gives the wine a purer taste with finesse and elegance.

Currently, Ooka only makes one wine from his own vines. That's his Cornas. The others are *négoce*—meaning he buys grapes from others and makes the wines. These come from biodynamic properties and are sold under the Le Canon label, totaling 30,000 bottles in all. He hopes one day to get rid of the Le Canon and concentrate on his Cornas, which would be a tremendous shame. It's a great opportunity to see the man's work at a convenient price point, even if we can't taste the specific taste of his personal plots of land. Our palates (and pocketbooks) would be sad to see the label disappear. I've been in love with these wines since he produced his first Le Canon vintage.

I first tasted Ooka's wines in 2003. They just seemed so very Cornas, animalistic and lively. Today, I still adore exploring and drinking all the wine he produces. But often my adoration of his wines is more passionate in France. I am on the fence about how well these wines travel to the United States. At times, their 100 percent gorgeousness seems impaired. But even at less than 100 percent perfection, they are worth the exploration if you can find and afford them. From the Le Canon Rouge to the Cornas, Ooka's wines range from $20 to $80.

WHO TO DRINK

- Franck Balthazar; Cornas (organic)
- La Grande Colline; Cornas (organic)
- Thierry Allemand; Cornas (organic)
- Augustus Clape; Cornas (organic)
- Marcel Juge; Cornas (sustainable)
- Michaël Bourg; Cornas (organic)
- Eric Texier/Domaine de Pergaud; Côte-Rôtie, Brézème (organic)
- Bernard Levet; Côte-Rôtie (sustainable)
- Jean-Michel Stephan; Côte-Rôtie (organic)
- Stéphane Otheguy; Côte-Rôtie (organic)
- Pierre Bénétière; Côte-Rôtie (organic)
- Dard & Ribo; Crozes-Hermitage, Saint-Joseph, Hermitage (organic)
- Domaine Jean Gonon; Saint-Joseph (organic)
- J-L Chave; Hermitage, Saint-Joseph (organic)
- Domaine des Miquettes/Paul Estève; Saint-Joseph (organic)

The Loire: Muscadet

Whether soils have any impact on wine flavor will forever be a hot debate as scientists try to quantify what winemakers and tasters know instinctively. But there are no better vineyards on Earth to shut down the naysayers than in the far west Loire, in the region of Pays Nantais lovingly referred to as the Muscadet. It is there that one of the Muscadet masters, Guy Bossard, the now-retired creator of Domaine de l'Ecu (taken over by Fred Niger van Herck) had this to say: "Refusing to recognize the impact of terroir on the personality of the wine is a serious mistake or bullshit!"

Indeed.

The Dirt

During the Precambrian Era, a huge sea upheaval coughed up mostly intrusive igneous and metamorphic material to land. This formed what is called the "Armorican Massif," the basement that underlies Brittany, Normandy, and the lower Loire Valley. Later on came the pressures and uplifts of metamorphics—schists and gneiss commingled with the volcanic matter. Fast forward a few million years and erosion flattened the area, which lies no more than perhaps 120 meters above sea level. So while you won't find the peaks and the heights of more dramatic regions, what it lacks in drops it more than makes up for in interesting weather and soils.

The land surrounding the city of Nantes is damp, windy, low land, and the soils are like gravelly dry curds. The grape that primarily grows there is the one the region takes its name for: Muscadet, or more correctly known as Melon de Bourgogne.

Considering some of my wine hotspots are the Alsace, northern Rhône, Sierra Nevada foothills, Beaujolais, and western Loire, I can easily draw the conclusion that I'm more than just a little fond of granite's effect on a vine. But why? What is it about a soil with a granitic profile?

In search of the answers, I went to talk to another granite lover, David Lillie, co-owner of the iconic Tribeca store Chambers Street Wines.

Lillie and I sat in the back of the shop one July afternoon while he recalled a visit to Muscadet master Marc Ollivier of Domaine de la Pépière. "Marc said to me that he made all of his wines from all of his plots the same way. The plots are very close to each other but all have different soils and all taste quite different. What's more is that as they age, their differences are even more apparent. To him that was the proof of terroir."

To illustrate, Lillie uncorked (and unscrewed) two wines of the same vintage. One was a Clos des Briords from Ollivier's small parcel on Château-Thébaud, replete with crumbly, silvery granite. The other was Jo Landron's Domaine de la Louvetrie Fief du Breil, grown on a hillside of the metamorphic orthogneiss with clay and small quartz.

"The aromatic difference between the two terroirs is in the quality of the acidity and aroma," said Lillie. He stuck his nose into the Briords. He pondered, then commented, "The first thing that I always seem to get from this wine is an atmospheric sense of freshness and acidity. No real fruit. But as the nose develops, I pick up a hint of white flower and lemon peel. Delicate citrus peel has relatively strong acidity, leaner. The orthogneiss gives more fat. People often say that they can smell rocks, but the smell is actually generated by acidity and is far less apparent in orthogneiss soils."

Just how well a grape will express the soil, David believes, is dependent on the farming. It is no surprise then that the resurrection of the depressed region that produces Muscadet owes everything to those who work biodynamically, organically, or at least responsibly. Among those who did the heavy lifting are Ollivier, Landron, Michel Brégeon, Guy Bossard, and Pierre Luneau-Papin. Good farming and practice has saved the Beaujolais as well, delivering it from the curse of the nouveau.

But sometimes terroir can triumph over chemicals, Lillie notes:

"There are examples in both Bordeaux and Burgundy where inert dead soils still remarkably produce good wine in spite of the farming." One reason, he said, is the enormously complicated chain of life in which organisms pass along the soil's nutrients. These are eventually picked up by mycorrhizal fungi and fed to the vine. Those complex chains don't exist to the same degree in a dead soil, but they do exist. So terroir, if it is great, can survive.

We then went to Landron's wine. The alcohols were identical at 12 percent, and both were bone dry. The Fief, grown on orthogneiss, hit with fruit and herbal notes and gave the impression of being riper and rounder. "There is lemon here as in the Briords, but it is a ripe, round lemon. You never perceive that round kind of aromatic and taste from any granite soil. The Fief will last, but it will not be as long-lived as the Briords."

Bossard offers these estimates about the aging: "Two to five years on gneiss. Four to eight years for orthogneiss. And from five to ad infinitum on granite."

The main terroir component delivered in the glass is the soil's impact on acidity expression. This was something that I hadn't really considered in its profundity until that afternoon with Lillie. Granite, for example, with its low pH, produces highly acidic wines. "We smell and taste types of acidity," says Lillie. "We experience it in the mouth and on the nose. We are not tasting the stone, or the granite, but tasting the effects of it."

So in answer to my question, why do I love granitic soils? I suppose it's because as a girl who thinks a lemon improves just about everything, it has to be in the acid.

The Grapes

There used to be plenty of red grapes grown in the eastern Loire, but that was before the big deep freeze of 1709. Now it is known as a white wine region, but as climate change is encroaching, the red plantings are creeping back. Here is some Cabernet Franc and Côt (Malbec) and a bit of Gamay and Pinot Noir. They're simple and satisfying. Now-retired Muscadet master Guy Bossard said that his Cabernet Franc on granite looked very much like the floral side of Pinot Noir. Meanwhile, the region is known for non-aromatic white grapes. One is Gros Plant, the local name for Folle Blanche. This is the very same grape that most often turns up in Armagnac. As a still wine, it struggles under the reputation of being a somewhat vile, acidic grape. But those who like their wine with edge will disagree and seek these out from organic or biodynamic producers, especially when it shows up as a sparkling wine. The other grape, however, is the defining one of the region. The Muscadet is, without a doubt, the territory of Melon de Bourgogne. As the name suggests, it most likely did come from Burgundy. Melon is highly suited to Pays Nantais because it's relatively sturdy in the area's cold winters. Jancis Robinson has been dismissive of it, saying "there is limited but marked enthusiasm for the variety in the US." Call us some of those with "marked enthusiasm."

Winemaking in the Muscadet

Traditional winemaking is simple: Raise and ferment in cement tanks, many submerged beneath the ground. On the label you'll see another clue, *sur lie*, which means "on the lees." This is the practice of leaving the wines to age on the spent lees until bottling. While this might seem like dirty winemaking, the nutrition in the spent lees brings a lot of depth, texture, flavor, and a touch of creaminess to the wine. Traditionally, malolactic fermentation does not occur, and most of the wines are bottled within a year. Yet there are exceptions. And today more ambitious producers are aging the wines longer in barrels, not in cement, allowing the malo to happen and a very different image of a rounder muscadet to emerge.

Deceptively simple, the grape is highly sensitive and expressive and can age far longer than its gentle pricing indicates. In addition, it is extremely place-sensitive and a great translator of soil. Lucky for us, here is a great opportunity to see what one grape can do from the same producer on different soils. They can be silver-tongued, edgy, refreshing wines with a lashing of salinity. They can be rounder and shorter. They can have vibrant electricity. Mostly, as David noted, what you'll find is how acidity is delivered to the palate depending on whether the grapes grew on amphibolite, schist, gneiss, or granite. There are some winemakers experimenting with Melon stateside, especially in Oregon, where you can experience it from basalt.

The Crus Communaux

The best growers of the Muscadet always knew they had something special, but for years, even those who worked organically and raised their wine traditionally in cement tanks (and made beautifully angular, salty wines) were only getting pennies for their heartfelt wines. Fed up, the Muscadet growers banded together to make a point. In 2011, the work of about 50 top growers resulted in a Grand Cru classification for Muscadet, called the Crus Communaux. The first ones to get the designation were Gorgeois on gabbro, Clisson on granite, and Le Pallet on orthogneiss and gabbro. Eventually, this should also go to Goulaine on mica schists and gneiss. (Note that gneiss, orthogneiss, schist, and amphibolite are metamorphic.)

The idea was to give credence to the Muscadets known for their richness, their complexity, and ageability. There would be some parameters such as limiting yields and minimum aging on the lees. The designation requires 17 to 24 months aging *sur lie*. Like everywhere else, they want an appellation status. Be prepared for a much deserved price increase.

INTRODUCING THE CRUS COMMUNAUX
1. Gorges (clay and quartz atop gabbro)
2. Le Pallet (metamorphic: gabbro, gneiss, and orthogneiss)
3. Clisson (granite)
4. Monnières-Saint Fiacre (metamorphic: gneiss)
5. Château-Thébaud (granite)
6. Goulaine (metamorphic: gneiss and schist)
7. Mouzillon-Tillières (metamorphic: gabbro)
8. La Haye-Fouassière (gneiss, orthogneiss, and amphibolites)
9. Vallet (metamorphic: schist with volcanic gabbro on the perimeter)

WHO TO DRINK

THE CLASSICS
- Domaine de la Louvetrie/Jo Landron; La Haye-Fouasière (biodynamic)
- Domaine de l'Ecu; Le Landreau (biodynamic)
- Marc Ollivier/Domaine de la Pépière; Maisdon-sur-Sevre (organic)
- Domaine Pierre Luneau-Papin; Le Landreau (biodynamic conversion)
- Jacques Carroget/Domaine de la Paonnerie (organic)
- André-Michel Brégeon & Frédéric Lailler/Domaine Michel Brégeon; Gorges (sustainable)
- Bruno Cormerais; Saint-Lumine-de Clisson (sustainable)

- Complémen'Terre/Manuel Landron & Marion Pescheux (organic)
- Vincent Caillé/Domaine Le Fay d'Homme; Monnières Saint Fiacre (organic)
- Jérôme Bretaudeau/Domaine de Bellevue; Gétigné (organic)
- Marc Pesnot/Domaine de la Sénéchalière; Le Loroux-Bottereau (organic)
- Julien Braud; Monnières Saint Fiacre (organic conversion)
- Domaine Bonnet-Huteau; La Chapelle-Heulin (organic, bio-dynamic)

Beaujolais

Imagine kicking your child out of the house and banishing her to a bare and rugged land to fend for herself in the cold and the rain. In this case, the child was the Gamay grape. The nasty parent was the land of Burgundy. Here's what happened:

Gamay first appeared in the 14th century, when the grape was noticed right outside Saint-Aubin in Burgundy in the town called Gamay. Like the new girl in town who turns everyone's head, the grape initially made a big splash. In his book *The Story of Wine*, writer Hugh Johnson reported that the people of the region considered the grape to be the Almighty's apology for the bubonic plague. The variety showed promise by bearing an abundant crop and ripening a full two weeks earlier than did the hometown favorite, Pinot Noir. The resultant wine also delivered plenty of flavor. But in 1395, the Duke of Burgundy, Philippe the Bold, called the Gamay vine a "bad and disloyal plant" whose wine was foul, bitter, and harmful to humans. My God! What slander. Finding that the vines lacked the aristocratic elegance, light texture, and fragrance of other wines in the region, he ordered that they be destroyed.

Yet the grape was a survivor and took up root in the Loire and the northern Rhône, as well as in Beaujolais. In those regions, it became the peasant queen. The grape was never viewed as royal. Farmers suffered. Caught between the grandeur of the northern Rhône and the regal Burgundy, Gamay and Beaujolais had awkward middle child syndrome.

Centuries later they suffered another abuse with the arrival of Beaujolais Nouveau. Created as a marketing spoof by Georges Dubœuf, the third Thursday of November was declared as the day this wine, the first peek at the new vintage, was shown to the world. Fanfare and parties ensued. The problem was, the wine was a parody of a real one. Oh, sure, it was a nice, easy drink, but it prevented most of the world from understanding just how good the grape on the granite in the windy microclimate on those hilly slopes can be. And so the world looked away from a region that had fallen into poverty and bad wines. Salvation came in the form of a winemaker named Marcel Lapierre. He lived in the village of Morgon and realized his wines and those of his friends were awful. As he told me years later, "The two tits of the Beaujolais were sulfur and sugar," referring to the fact that the grapes were picked underripe, then fermented with sugar and then sulfited to keep the wines stable. All in all, a toxic stew. With the help of a naturally minded scientist and winemaker, a gentleman named Jules Chauvet, Lapierre started to farm organically and make wine naturally, even leaving out the sulfur. His friends caught on. The winemakers became known as the Band of Five, first sold to Paris, and then in the '80s, to the rest of the world.

As one friend told another, and that friend told another, the trend spread until something referred to as the natural wine movement took hold and changed the way the whole world was drinking. These were serious wines with deep traditional roots. Mostly they were made in semi-carbonic style, as was the custom. This meant instead of crushing the grapes, they were vinified in vats of whole berries. The fruit starts to ferment inside in an enzymatic fermentation that fosters fruity and spicy aromas. The wine is often thought of as not necessarily ready to drink early, but certainly ready by November.

Beaujolais had a lot in common with the Muscadet: Both were poor. Both had farmers that had a tough time making a living and even a good deal of suicides. But the natural winemakers in both regions found their drinkers and their fame. These are the wines I love to drink, yet only now are they getting respect.

Caught between the Syrah grown in the northern Rhône and the Pinot in Burgundy, Beaujolais's Gamay suffers. It has a far more subtle beauty but it sure does gorgeously on granite.

The Dirt

In the south of Beaujolais, the soil is derived from limestone and contains quite a bit of clay, dismissed as just not good for Gamay, but there are a few exquisite examples that contradict this. Gamay on granite tends to be edgier and more acidic and tends to do better in the cold and damp. Limestone, depending on the clay content, tends to be a bit fleshier and does better in the dry and hot. It is also there that the Chardonnay is mostly grown to produce the little-known Beaujolais Blanc. The more well-known regions are in the north, where there's a powerful granite spine and where all the ten crus exist (more on these below). But nevertheless, the takeaway is that this is the land where granite pays homage to the grape. And the others are fabulous exceptions.

There are ten special places for Beaujolais, and these are called the "crus." Each of these villages has their specific nuances, and create structured wines of beauty that have that touchstone of breeding and the ability to age very well. The look of the vines in the region is compelling as well. They are not conventionally trellised, but grow in petite round bushes that are almost bonsai-like. Each cru has its own distinct soil profile:

Saint-Amour: Granite and clay

Juliénas: Sand-like granite on the west; gneiss and schist, with some veins of manganese and porphyry, and alluvial with more clay on the east

Chiroubles: One of the highest crus, granite and clay smectite

Chénas: Pink granite, red sand, and quartz

Moulin-à-Vent: The pinkest granite

Fleurie: Another high-elevation cru, pink granite with some clay

Morgon: Mostly schist with important patches of granite

Régnié: Sand-like granite and schist

Brouilly: Pink and blue intrusive igneous rocks, granite, diorite, schist (pierre bleue), limestone, and sandstone

Côte-de-Brouilly: Pink and blue intrusive igneous rocks, pink granite on the west, blue diorite on the north and south

The Grapes

During the harvest that I worked at Clos Roche Blanche in the Loire, I picked Gamay from limestone. My hands were inked black from the grapes—thin-skinned and juicy, their pigment is fierce. Gamay has quite a tight bunch and is prone to rot, early to bud and early to ripen. It also is a sloppy mess if grown in too sunny a land, as it is susceptible to sunburn. For this reason, it seems to do perfectly well in the difficult, windy, and often wet and dreary Beaujolais. And the taste? Well, think of Pinot Noir: delicate, some tannins, and yet marvelously hinting of forest fruit. It is in the same family of, dare I say, feminine wines, easy to drink without being stupid. The traditional semi-carbonic method gives it a cinnamon flavor and aroma, but it often has some delicate sandpaper tannin. In the northern Rhône, there are barely any vines left, but worth drinking if you can find them. In the Loire, on just about any of the soils there (limestone, basalt, and schist), it is often easygoing and more grounded. It's gaining popularity in Oregon and there's a bit of a rush on it in California. Planted in the right places and perhaps blended with Cabernet Franc, as can be the case in the Loire, it can shine. It was in the granite belt of Australia, in Beechworth, that I once had a strikingly lovely Gamay from Barry Morey of Sorrenberg. Was it a combination of the poor granite soils that were not irrigated and careful biodynamic farming that made this grape possible over there? Was it the marriage of place, soil, and farmer? The vintage I tasted was made without sulfur addition and was more than 20 years old. It had structure. It had fruit. It had integrity. The wine maintained everything that allowed a wine to be called agreeable. I was impressed. Though little of it is made, there is Chardonnay, and usually what is made is quite good. The best are made gently with no fanfare and they are often good bargains. Definitely look for those from Jean-Paul Brun (Domaine des Terres Dorées), Christophe Pacalet, Jean-Paul Dubost, and Pierre Chermette.

Winemaker Profile: Domaine de la Grand'Cour

Jean-Louis Dutraive worked with his father from 1977, but took over the Domaine de la Grand'Cour in Fleurie in 1989. For a while, the wines had been earning dubious reviews from both Robert Parker and David Schildknecht. But in all fairness, perhaps *The Wine Advocate* hadn't been aware of a dramatic change. Dutraive has been certified by the organic expert body ECOCERT since 2009, which was also his first year of working differently. I asked him why he changed. After all, with due respect, he's not exactly a spring chicken, and at this point in life, most people have settled into their work philosophy. His reasoning was simple: "I tasted other wines that had more life in them, and so I started to work more naturally."

Dutraive returned to full carbonic fermentation (dump whole grape clusters into a vat, seal it up, add CO_2, and let the fermentation start from within the berry). He employed a combination of stainless steel, old big barrels, and small *barriques* of various ages. He bottled his wine unfiltered with minimal SO_2 added (sometimes with none at all). Vines have an average age of around 40 to 50 years, with a good chunk around 70 years old, which is moderately old for the region. He has about nine hectares, the majority of which is on the granitic soils of Fleurie, in Le Clos, right near his winery. The others are in two small parcels. There is an additional 1.6 hectares in Brouilly limestone.

After driving through Le Clos, I reached Dutraive's run-down farm buildings, where an eager dog came out yapping at me. A quick peek into the weary vines (rot, uneven maturity), proved a little depressing. It was a difficult year, especially for those working the vines. Just the day before, I had read dire predictions: 50 percent of the Beaujolais vignerons would be going under because of the difficult weather and low yields. But I believe those unfortunates are mostly those with little reputation for quality. Even though the region is on the upswing, thanks to serious winemakers like Dutraive, Beaujolais still has plenty of underachieving vineyards and winemakers.

In the Clos, Dutraive told me that he would soon be down to 15 hectoliters per hectare, a ludicrously low yield in a region where 60 is normal. He shrugged it off. This is what he signed up for with organic farming. He might not have much to sell in 2012, but he had enough in 2011, and there's always the next year—and he's a vigneron with a reputation on the ascent.

With the dog riding shotgun, Dutraive brought us through the large vat room, lined with variously sized barrels, many of them the very large ovals. We sat down at a rough-hewn table and commenced to taste.

The wines are gorgeous. Clos de la Grand'Cour is made from younger vines (ten years), has a touch of sulfur (2 ppm). It's structured and silty, with a bite of blood orange. For me, the heartthrob wines came from older vines. A no-sulfur-added bottling of Chapelle des Bois, raised in the bigger-than-Bordeaux-sized barrels they call *foudre*, had a slightly gritty texture, a touch of cinnamon aroma, and mouthwatering acidity. It practically shouted its place of origin. Next, we tried the Cuvée Champagne Vieilles Vignes, hailing from very granitic soils from the *lieu-dit* "Champagne" (even though it is not a Premier Cru or Grand Cru). In this wine, the structure shines. It also takes a little new wood, which seemed integrated to me. The Brouilly Vieilles Vignes comes from very different soils of clay and limestone. Accordingly, the texture was denser, with the characteristic savory/fruit balance of that combination.

Three days after being opened, the wines still held together.

The last time I went to see Dutraive, I was with Pascaline. It was the winter. The dog still came out to bark at me, but his master seemed a little unnerved. I pointed to a burned-out building, and he shook his head. He had been up battling the fires all night and had forgotten about our visit. But with an "oh well," a smile, and all of his good nature, we went to taste.

WHO TO DRINK

- Domaine des Vignes du Mayne/Julien Guillot; Beaujolais Village (biodynamic)
- Yohan Lardy; Moulin a Vent (organic)

- Damien Coquelet; Chiroubles (sustainable, organic)
- Clos de la Roilette; Fleurie (sustainable)
- Yann Betrand; Fleurie, Morgon (organic)
- Yvon Métras; Fleurie (biodynamic)
- Jean Foillard; Morgon, Fleurie (organic)
- Juien Sunier; Régnie, Fleurie, Morgon (organic)
- Domaine de la Grand'Cour; Fleurie, Brouilly (organic)
- Karim Vionnet; Morgon (organic)
- Domaine J. Chamonard; Morgon, Fleurie (organic)
- Marcel Lapierre; Morgon (organic, biodynamic)
- Louis Claude Desvignes; Morgon (sustainable)
- Antoine Sunier; Régnié (organic)
- Domaine Ducroux; Régnié (biodynamic)
- Domaine Pignard; Régnié, Morgon (biodynamic)
- Jean Paul & Charly Thevenet; Morgon, Régnié (organic)
- Georges Descombes; Brouilly (organic)
- Clotaire Michel; Beaujolais (organic)
- Marcel Joubert; Brouilly, Morgon, Chiroubles, Fleurie (organic)
- Rémy Dufaitre; Brouilly (organic)
- Domaine des Terres Dorées; Charnay (organic)

Rías Baixas

If French Muscadet has a Spanish counterpart it would be Albariño, the wine from the northwest of Spain that's oh-so-close to the top of Portugal. The top winemaking region here is Galicia, and specifically Rías Baixas.

The Dirt

Rías Baixas is a land of pink quartz-flecked granitic soils where you're never too far from the ocean. Drive around and take in the granite poles supporting old vines in traditional pergola training, where the vines create an netting overhead, high above the grass below. This keeps the grapes safe from the constant threat of mildew from the humidity. Up there, they can dry out in the Atlantic winds. Like Muscadet, the wines have a delicious salinity, and also like Muscadet, it's best to vinify them simply. Unlike Muscadet, where fermentation often happens in old concrete vats, the best wines here are likely made in old, large, and neutral oak barrels, that do not (or should not) impart any taste, but round out the angles of this high-acid wine.

The Grapes

Albariño is the region's calling card. True, it is said that its origin is actually across the border in Portugal, where it's called Alvarinho, but that's splitting hairs. Some red varieties are grown here, just like some red grapes are grown in the Muscadet. Here, the red varieties of choice are Caíño, Espadeiro, and Mencía. Just like in the Muscadet, as climate change goes into effect and the region gets warmer and drier, the reds will encroach even further into this 90 percent white wine territory.

Albariño is a relatively thick-skinned grape that loves dry soil. You might think that wet Galicia would be a bad fit, but that's where the granitic soil comes in. Sometimes it's mixed with clay, which is just fine in a drought, but in a wet climate, well-drained granitic soils saves Albariño. It is grown a tiny bit in California, with decent results, but nowhere else other than Rías Baixas will you get the edge of the northern coast of Iberia. Because it could well be considered a neutral grape—much like Muscadet—comparisons have been made to Riesling, which is kind of silly. But left to its own devices, Albariño's true nature can take on notes of linden and gentle spring flowers in the distance, and these only get more profound with a little age. It is from the land and hands of Alberto Nanclares that the grace of the area is exemplified.

Winemaker profile: Alberto Nanclares

Alberto Nanclares was once an economist. He moved to Rías Baixas in 1993 to be near the sea. The house he bought was in Cambados, in the high-potential viticultural area of Val do Salnés. It had vines. Nanclares slowly gave in to the plants that would soon overtake his life. At first, he used chemicals in the vines, but he quickly realized his folly and stopped. He started to make wine with an enologist. The enologist instructed him to remove the acid, which he felt made the wine shrill. At that point Nanclares said, "to hell with you," and kept his natural acids. After that, he made wine on his own.

Today, Nanclares has 2.5 hectares of Albariño vines that are broken into twelve different parcels. He makes five wines from them: two blends and three single-vineyard bottlings. He farms organically. His yields are low: 4,000 to 7,000 kilograms per hectare instead of the 12,000 allowed by the DO. Walking out into the bright sunshine, less than a mile from the sea, it's a cinch to suss out the difference between his path and his neighbors': life. As we walked and his dogs romped around us, the wild mint and brilliant dandelion crushed under our feet exuded the intense essence of spring.

The soils are typical of the region's best: clay, sand, and fragments of granite. All of his parcels are vinified separately and all of his vines are traditional pergola. Nanclares described the wisdom of the trained high trellising as opposed to the *guyot*, the more typical trellising closer to the ground, which many of the new plantings in the region use. With pergola, there's more humidity control, and you don't need to prune as severely. We went down to examine the vineyard right near the river on his property where, because of the fine, sandy soils, the drainage is efficient—important in a very wet, soggy area like Galicia. The area creates grapes with high acidity, which makes the natural process of malolactic fermentation malfunction, and so the grapes here most often fail to complete it and maintain their natural angularity. If you remember the aging potential of great Muscadets, you'll want to get some of these to lay into your cellar, maybe not for twenty years, but certainly up to ten.

As we started to taste through his cuvées, he reminisced about his 2013 vintage. In that year, there was a relentless rain, even at harvest, which is always panic-inducing. At the time, he says, "I wanted to cry. But now? I'm happy!" And so are the wines, which are saline, edgy, full of spark and personality.

THE IGNEOUS TASTING BOX

To get the full impression of the potential of wine from fire-born rocks, you'll want an assortment of wines grown on granite and basalt. Here are a few bottles that are fine representations:

1. Marc Ollivier/Domaine de la Pépière, Granite de Clisson; Muscadet, Loire, France (granite)

The first impression for this wine from the Melon grape is freshness and a green apple acidity. There's no real fruit to speak of, but as the nose develops, I pick up hints of white flower and lemon peel. Delicate citrus peel reflects relatively strong lemon. There are almost no tannins and a

salty, lingering finish, which can reach such a concentration you might mistake it for mineral water.

2. Alberto Nanclares, Dandelion; Rías Baixas, Galicia, Spain (granite)

This Albariño has a lot in common with the Pépière; neutrality on the nose and a taste that stretches wide in the mouth. It then hits with a delicious, mouth-watering lime acidity that starts to spread. Like the Pépière, there's also a smooth texture and a finish like a briny stone. Unlike the Pépière, there's more power and more of an oiliness, with touches of exotic lemongrass and orange blossom.

3. Salvo Foti/I Vigneri, Aurore; Etna Bianco Superiore, Sicily, Italy (basalt and black scoria)

A rare Carricante, a beautiful little grape grown in sight of the ocean, on a land with plenty of sun. Here, there's an orange-like acidity and smell. The taste hits with a fierce, rusty edge, and gives over to a very refreshing tension that is felt on the sides of the tongue, ending in a long finish.

4. Haridimos Hatzidakis, Assyrtiko de Mylos; Santorini, Greece (white pumice and ash)

Another seaside selection is the grape Assyrtiko, which hails from white sandy soils. The lemon is here, the attack is fierce. But there is also such fierce acidity, puckery, and cleansing acids, a little bit like a scrubbing. The most tannic of all of the wines listed here, with an almond skin quality giving a lot of texture to the wine. With a higher level of alcohol, it is a big boy.

5. **Calabretta, Etna Rosso; Sicily, Italy (basalt and scoria)**

This red wine from Mount Etna has a lot in common with the other seaside representatives. A blend of Nerello Mascalese and Nerello Cappuccio, the soils it grows in are lower in elevation and less sandy. But the acidity is not subtle; it comes at the end like an ashen rasp of the hammer. There's some sesame seed, some linseed, and underneath it all, some blackcurrant.

6. **Domaine Marcel Joubert, Fleurie Vieilles Vignes; Beaujolais, France (pink granite and clay)**

Tannin at the finish on top of apple-like acid. The fruit takes a backseat to the savory and it is just a completely satisfying Beaujolais. Note how there's definitely that fruit but there's a frame around it, a structure that's a little gritty and yet transparent. It all knits together and a story unfolds of fresh spring, concentration, and just a little bit of fur.

7. **Jason Lett/The Eyrie Vineyards, Pinot Noir Reserve Original Vines; Dundee Hills, Oregon (Jory)**

The Eyrie Pinot is one of the most transparent in Oregon—ungrafted vines and definitely an age-worthy one. With a noticeable upfront ripeness, the tannins are a little more assertive and broad than in Burgundy, almost giving a nebbiolesque-feel with age—smoky, pastrami-like. The acid is here, ripe yet fierce, and holding up very well with the alcohol and the touch of vegetal green.

8. **Hervé Souhaut/Domaine Romaneaux-Destezet; Saint-Joseph, Northern Rhône, France (degraded granite)**

Gentle smell of smoke and a little bit of berry. In the mouth, the Syrah shows its acidity from the front. In the back, there's spark and energy.

The body is medium and limpid, and there's a bit of wet nail as well; the tannins are quite subtle.

Are all of these grapes, white or red, as dissimilar as you think?

Acids: Where do they hit your mouth? Are they sharp, soft, difficult, juicy?

Tannins: Are they harsh? Ripe? Suede-like? Sandpapery? An ash-like finish?

Taste: Savory? Briny? Spicy? Flinty?

Texture: Grainy or smooth?

Structure: What is it like? Is there one? An exoskeleton? Or more of an interior scaffolding?

Igneous Cheat Sheet

Where	Soils	Climate	Known For
France: Loire, Muscadet	granite	mild winters, warm summers; humid and western wind	Melon
France: Beaujolais	granite	continental	Gamay, Chardonnay
France: Northern Rhône	granite	cold winter, warm summer	Syrah, Viognier, Marsanne, Roussanne
Greece: Santorini	pumice, volcanic	windy, hot	Assyrtiko
Spain: Canary Islands	basalt	tropical with a lot of variation depending on altitude	Negramoll, Listán Negro and Blanco

Spain: Galicia	granite	cool, wet	Albariño
Spain: Ribeira Sacra	granite, metamorphic schist	cool, wet	Mencía, Godello, Treixadura, Lado, Ferrol, Caiño, Garnacha Tintorera
Spain: Sierra de Gredos	granite	hot, dry	Albillo, Garnacha
Italy: Mount Etna	basalt, ash	hot, sun	Nerello Mascalese, Cappuccio, Carricante
Italy: Bramaterra	granite, tuff	damp mountain climate	Croatina, Uva Rara
Italy: Soave	basalt, limestone	wet and temperate	Garganega
Hungary: Tokaj	basalt, tuff	continental— harsh cold winter, warm summer	Hárslevelü, Furmint
Australia: Beechworth	granite	hot, dry	Syrah, Pinot Noir, Gamay, Chardonnay
USA: Willamette, Oregon	basalt	wet, sunny	Pinot Noir
USA: Sierra Nevada foothills, California	granite	high elevation, hot, dry	Syrah, Mourvèdre, Gamay
USA: Vermont	granite, schist	cool, wet	Marquette, Louise Swenson, Frontenac

CHAPTER 2

SEDIMENTARY

Do you know that sludge left in the bottom of the glass after you finish an old bottle of Burgundy? This is wine sediment, the slurry of the wine that fell to the bottom. This is the way sedimentary rock is formed but under the complications of pressure and time.

The slurry from bodies of water ranging from creeks to oceans, compressed over eons, turns into sedimentary rock. This category includes all sorts of fun things, from sooty coal to mystical amber. But when it comes to the dirt that suits the vine, it is the dark shale, the lively limestone, the desert-evoking sandstone, the durable flint (silex), and magical diatomite that fascinate. Textures are also important and they too fall under the rubric of sedimentary soil. These include the *galets* rocks of Chateauneuf-du-Pape and Rioja, as well as the petite gravels of Bordeaux, Napa, and New Zealand. And then there's the loess of Austria and California. The category is tremendously diverse.

SANDSTONE: Most sandstone is composed of quartz and/or feldspar. These are the most common minerals in the Earth's crust. Like sand, sandstone comes in many shades; the color depends on the mineral content. The most prevalent hues are tan, brown, yellow, red, gray, pink, white, and black. Sandstone beds often form highly visible cliffs and other topographical features. The notable sandstone regions are parts of Alsace, Piemonte, Chianti, and the eastern parts of the country of Georgia.

SILEX: When quartz-like silicon dioxide goes through not compression but chemical changes, it emerges into a metal-like hardness called silex, more commonly known as flint or chert. This stone gave humankind our first sharp blades for slicing and hunting. It's an incredibly hard rock that, when smashed, fragments into painfully sharp edges. It forms when caught up in limestone or chalk, and that is why it exists almost exclusively where limestone is found. But there are a few vineyard spots in the world where its presence is profound. The notable flinty wine regions are in the Loire and especially certain terroirs in Sancerre and Touraine.

SHALE: Like slate, shale is dark and layered. But this most common type of sedimentary rock did not go through the heat of metamorphism, only the pressure. And so this is a sedimentary compressed mud with a bit of quartz and other minerals. Notable regions include Montalcino, parts of Tuscany (where it's called *galestro*), the Finger Lakes in New York, part of the Swartland around Malmesbury in South Africa, and parts of Santa Barbara, California.

DIATOMITE: Never heard of diatomite? Of course you have, but probably by another name: diatomaceous earth. It's everywhere in our life, from cat litter to water filtration to toothpaste. This soft rock is made of compressed diatoms and the fossils of algae and other creatures. White as chalk, but without any carbonate calcium content, it is almost pure silica with very little organic matter. While it is quite rare, you can find some in California, both in Santa Barbara and in the Santa Rita hills near Lompoc.

LIMESTONE: This sedimentary soil formed from ancient seabeds and coral reefs has given birth to such revered and profound wine regions that sometimes I think Neptune not only rules over the sea but also the vine. Pascaline and I could write three books about the limestone regions that make great wine, so compressing it down to just a few pages is a challenge. But nevertheless, at the top of the heap, the sediments that bring winemakers and drinkers to their knees are the white and yellow, chalky, porous, sponge-like limestone. There are some evangelists who consider this the high emperor of rocks.

LIMESTONE

There are many uses for this sedimentary rock, ranging from flooring to scrubbing an amphora. But it's so intrinsically linked to great wine that I had to laugh when I once read this definition of limestone: "A hard sedimentary rock, composed mainly of calcium carbonate or dolomite, used as building material and in the making of cement."

Technically, limestone is merely a rock, one made of the minerals calcite and aragonite. But spiritually? Ooh la la. To some, it's the holiest vine soil going. It is associated with elegance. Limestone is something that you first sense up front in the mouth, on the tip of the tongue, and it betokens a long finish with a linear structure. From dense limestone to chalk, these soils formed from the decomposed bodies of all kinds of creatures, from mollusks to fishes to coral. The most notable limestone soils are the brilliant white, chalky (complicated with plenty of diatomite) *albariza* in Spain's Jerez region, yellow and white tuffeau in the Loire, the gray and white chalk in Champagne, and the limestone in Burgundy.

Limestone in its purest state is white or almost white. But like a white dress where every stain is easily seen, the elements that mix with the limestone cause many limestones to sport different hues, especially on weathered soils.

According to Tablas Creek, a California winery that went out of its way to locate and plant on limestone in the Golden State, there is increasing evidence that calcium-rich soils help maintain acidity in grapes late in the growing season, as long as what's planted there are the right grapes. Calcium also is purported to strengthen the grape against certain diseases.

These are fantastic bonuses, but the real benefit lies in the soil's water-retention capabilities—especially where people dry farm. Water is necessary for the essential processes by which plants take up nutrients through their roots. Grapevines don't do well in waterlogged soils, which increase the likelihood of root disease. But with calcium-rich soil, the soils can hold the water, allowing the vine to drink instead of sitting in a pool of water, permitting the soil to retain moisture in periods of dry weather but allowing for good drainage during heavy rains. However, there are many variables that must be taken into consideration, such as slope and the percentage of clay minerals in the soil and whether there's a depression in the earth, where the water pools, or a cold spot, a hot wind, or a dry wind. But even with the extra factors, for many, limestone is the holy grail.

Soil scientists Claude and Lydia Bourguignon are limestone fanatics. I saw them speak several times, but the most memorable instance was in Switzerland, where Claude was quite the vision, with cowboy boots, flashing silver rings, and all around looking decidedly un-Burgundian, as he pronounced that "Seven percent of the Earth's geology is limestone; 55 percent of that is in Burgundy."

His figures have been debated by at least one notable geologist, but nevertheless, speaking in machine-gun-fast English, Bourguignon described the layout of Burgundy and the properties of different areas that gave rise to distinct traditions: "In Burgundy, the cooler and higher elevation is in the Côte de Nuits and it is more suitable for reds. The Côte de Beaune is warmer, and for some reason more suitable for whites. The monks knew what they were doing, as they made their decisions based on the quality of the soil, the quality of the mineral [limestone] content of the clay."

Bourguignon said there were really only two types of wines: wines of technology and wines of terroir. When it comes to the terroir, the land aspect, he said, should trump climate. "Climate will change over time, for sure, but year to year, the soil is more constant." The natural approach, with the least intervention you can get away with, is the only path to express terroir, he argued. He and I might disagree on the supremacy of limestone, but we do agree on farming methods. Natural practices make for a more active root system and a livelier soil where the nutrients from the ground, in all of their peculiarities, are more accessible to the plant. Of course, (and his last name has nothing to do with it) the best place for that soil is none other than Burgundy, France.

Burgundy

The first time I visited the holy land of Burgundy, I rode in on horseback.

Okay, that's a lie. I rode the train from Paris and arrived on a raw November day when the vines were bare. On solid ground in the town of Beaune, I felt quivery, starstruck. I am not alone in this reaction. People often kneel and kiss the soil upon their first visit. They take pictures at the vineyards. They steal grapes and leaves and rocks as souvenirs. The vines are tormented by paparazzi. People have even held them hostage, so valuable are they.

I have never been one for hero worship, but I was touched by the land's heritage and what it stood for. In modern times, the whole debate over terroir and matters of place started here.

The Romans first put down the vines in Burgundy, but it was the Cistercians who brought it to high art. In 775 CE, King Charlemagne put the land in the monks' stewardship, and over next 1000 years, the holy men plotted and assessed the land, tasting the soil along the way to perceive the differences. They developed a system of vineyard designation that became the gold standard around the world, distinguishing hundreds of plots they called *climats*. With Burgundy's subtle soil differences that change every few inches, every collector in the world will swear to you that they know how to blind taste a Vosne against a Volnay and a Charmes from a Chambertin. What makes one plot of land different from the other?

The Dirt

To understand what makes Burgundy soil so revered, time travel is needed, back to when the future famed region was a hot and humid land located near the Earth's equator. The sea soon swallowed the tropical mass whole when tectonic plates shifted. It was about 200 million years ago, during the Jurassic Period, when seashells and the remains of algae, fish, corals, and other organisms living in the tropical waters sank to the sea bottom. Over millions of years, their sediments created layers upon layers. Each layer had a different chemistry and a different texture. Pascaline thinks of this as a mille-feuille pastry, where some layers are harder and some are soggier.

A mere 140 million years later, the land was spit out from the water, only to discover the Earth was still in a tropical haze. The foundation of limestone was forming, but the land was not finished. First, the Alps had to be born. The peaks were born through the movement of plates, and from there commenced a series of bending and fracturing throughout the land. The Jura and Burgundy split from each other, creating the Saône fault, and lo and behold, up came this great and eventually famous limestone slope, with its variation of *climats*.

Not all of Burgundy is that perfect mix of limestone and clay (*argilocalcaire*). In fact, it is only in the Côte d'Or where that sublime, elastic kind of combination exists.

Burgundy's heart is the Côte d'Or, the slope of gold, a 35-mile stretch winding down south from Dijon. There are two lobes to that holy land: the Côte de Nuits, mostly famed for red, and the Côte de Beaune, famed for white. The road that runs through it from Dijon to Maranges was the long-celebrated RN74. Post-EU, it is called the D974. What hasn't changed is that it is built on the fault that divides the great terroir from the common. To the east, on the side of the railroad tracks, there's much more clay and less limestone, and it is too fertile and flat for great wine. That's where they grow wines called Passetoutgrains (Pinot and Gamay), Bourgogne Aligoté, and some basic Bourgogne red and white. There's not much of it, and if you wander, you'll soon be outside of vineyards into fields of cattle and grain.

The foundation for the great wines is toward the sunset and the cliffs. And on the slopes it is the middle section, the interior of a sandwich, so to speak, where the choicest spots lie. Thank you, medieval Cistercian monks, for figuring that out.

Those familiar with the huge vineyards of the New World would view Burgundy's crazy quilt patchwork of vines as quaint and insignificant. There are no huge vineyards here, but rather an endless stretch of small plots—the result of Napoleonic laws of inheritance. Most have many owners, sometimes with claimants even dividing rows within a vineyard. Then there are the rare exceptions, called *monopoles* (one vineyard, one owner, such as Frédéric Mugnier's Clos de la Maréchale in Nuits-Saint-Georges and Domaine de la Romanée-Conti's La Tâche and Romanée-Conti).

When last counted, the Côte d'Or had 32 Grands Crus—a designation reserved for the finest (and the most expensive) wines—and more than 460

Premiers Crus, the next step down. The slope is divided into two sections. The southern side is the Côte de Beaune, which hugs the city of Beaune, and stretches from Ladoix-Serrigny to Maranges. Then there's the more northern Côte de Nuits, which centers around the village of Nuits-Saint-George, and stretches south to Corgoloin and north to Marsannay. While their weather is similar, there are differences mostly in the clay mineral content, which is heavier in the north, making it more suitable for red grapes. The slopes are softer in Beaune and there are more different kinds of microclimates and open valleys, which might be the reason that Côte de Beaune is far more susceptible to damaging summer hails.

Burgundy's Hierarchy of Wine Labels

- At the top are the 33 Grands Crus, this includes one in Chablis
- Beneath them are the 570 Premiers Crus, including more than 460 in the Côte d'Or
- In the next step down, the bottle will sport a generic village name like Chorey-les-Beaunne, with no sign of Grand Cru or Premier Cru on the label
- Then there are generic Côte de Beaune or Côte de Nuits labels, from grapes within the district or subregions
- At the very bottom are the basic Burgundy labels; in this group are also Bourgogne Passetoutgrain, which is Gamay and Pinot and Bourgogne Aligoté; grapes can come from Chablis and Maçon and be blended

The Grapes

Burgundy's Côte d'Or is known for being a two-grape town: Pinot Noir and Chardonnay. Well, that's almost true. Back in the old Roman days, there was a multitude of grapes, including the mother of them all, Gouais Blanc. But we believe that it was the vine-tending monks who started to select and focus the breeding, and now, there's just a handful of varieties. The two major ones are those you really need to know for Wine 101: Pinot Noir and Chardonnay. For extra credit, read on.

PINOT NOIR: Burgundy has always been the most sublime expression of the neurotic Pinot Noir grape. Early budding makes this one a real loser if there's a freak frost. In rain and humidity, it's prone to rot. Thin-skinned, it splits easily, gets burnt, and remains pale in the glass. But when it all works, the world celebrates. Soils matter to this nervous vine, and it does love limestone. In Burgundy's long, cool growing seasons, the vine brings forth pretty, berry-like fruits; aromas of raspberry and red currants, and rosiness like that of Chanel No. 5 emerge. Other spots in France (the Loire, Jura, Alsace, Champagne) do beautifully with the grape, often on limestone as well. Want to see Pinot in other climes and soils? Pfalz in Germany has both limestone and basalt. In California, look to the shale of Santa Cruz and the diatomaceous soils of Lompoc, or on the loam of Sonoma. But in those sunny climates, especially when the soils are rich with loam, be prepared for a fruit bomb. Oregon's weather is a bit kinder to Pinot, but when the soil is volcanic (and note there are other soils there, such as sedimentary-rock based and others from flood deposits), the expression is less jam and more of an extreme sweetness of fruit.

GAMAY: Poor Gamay, banished from the best slopes to the heavy clay, allowed only to be mixed in with Pinot Noir for Passetoutgrain, or to be bottled all by itself in the Hautes Côtes, where they can be structured and refined. Go back and read all about it in the Beaujolais section on page 94.

CHARDONNAY: In the '90s, "I'll have your Chardonnay" became code for "White wine, please." And most of the world forgot that it was Burgundy that made some of the world's most famous white wines, like Montrachet and Chassagne-Montrachet. Soon, they were growing it everywhere, even in Rioja and in Piemonte. It was ludicrous. But Chardonnay is easy to grow, and because it's actually relatively neutral, you can put it in tons of makeup and dress it up any way you like. Ah, but to make it without tricks? Then you are left with a grape that can expose your farming ability.

Left to its own devices, Chardonnay has very little aroma and tends to a generous mouthfeel. It can be refreshing, tending toward lemony in cool climates and going tropical in the heat. There are some interesting clones. One is the rosy-colored grape, Chardonnay Rose. It's worth seeking out. This is another limestone-loving grape, with the world's finest examples coming from the Jura and Champagne. But on granite, it also manages to become less fleshy and more stately.

ALIGOTÉ: Not the vine for those who need immediate gratification. A vine has to be at least 15 years old before it gives anything good, but when it does, it sure does. It's a cousin of Chardonnay, and has been abused just as Gamay was—banished to the wrong side of the tracks. It tends to give a tart white wine. If you farm pitifully, you'll get an anemic, scratchy wine with screaming acidity. And that's how Aligoté became infamous for being the base for kirs, the wine mixed with crème de cassis. But give it low yields, organic farming, and the best limestone and clay marls Burgundy has to offer, and then this ugly duckling of a grape can take on the best. In fact, it was completely regal on a Grand Cru, the hill of Corton, up until 1972. With Jean-Charles le Bault de la Morinière, I had a forty-year-old stunner. Laurent Ponsot has made a very big point by making a Premier Cru Aligoté with his Les Monts Luisants, teaching us the lesson that it's the place that can bring out the best in a grape. Aligoté is not grown too many other places in the world. In Burgundy it has to have the grape name on the label, and it's called Bourgogne Aligoté, even if it comes from century-old vines in Chablis, as with Alice et Olivier de Moor. It has its own appellation, Bouzeron, located not in the fancy Côte d'Or but in the more plebeian Côte Chalonnaise. There's a little bit of it grown in the country of Georgia, on limestone soils in Switzerland, and there are also a few vines in California from Josh Jensen's Calera.

Other grapes commonly found in Burgundy are Pinot Gris, Pinot Beurot, Sauvignon Blanc, and César, which is a rustic red grape only allowed in the north, in Yonne. You'll never find them as single varieties, except under the Vin de France label and up in Auxerre, near Chablis. That's where Saint-Bris is an original appellation dedicated to Sauvignon Blanc.

Winemaker Profile: Domaine Bizot (Côte de Nuits)

I waited near the church in the hallowed village of Vosne-Romanée. This is the same village where Domaine de la Romanée-Conti exists, along with so many other famous names. This was the village with the most wine paparazzi and the most revered appellations of them all. An acre of land goes for well over a million dollars, though it never comes on the market. If you inherit land, like Jean-Yves Bizot did, that's the best way to get into this hallowed ground. Sighting Bizot, I waved to him and walked to greet the vigneron. He was tall and lanky, like an overgrown Harry Potter. "The vines?" I asked, eagerly.

Bizot had a patch right near his home, and we stepped in for a peek. It had been a very wet year, and it was nearing harvest time. He pulled back a stray vine and tucked it around a wire with an audible grunt: "Can you tell how fed up I am with them this year?"

We were just west of the road that used to be the RN74, in Les Jachées, a village-level vineyard. Our plan was to visit, taste, and have dinner with him and like-minded vigneronne, Claire Naudin, at their home in Vosne. But first, a moment of silence. All around us, in his and other vineyards, were the signs of the 2012 Burgundian summer of ten plagues. Cold. Hot. Hail. Rain. Mildew. Rot. Frogs. Slime. Boils. More Rot. It was hell if you worked organically, which is Bizot's way, though his vines are not certified.

Bizot originally studied geology, but when no one in his family wanted to take over the family vines, he stepped in. The year was 1993, and his first vintage was in 1995. "I had to unlearn everything I was taught in the Lycée Viticole," he said to me when I first met him, over eggplant curry in his kitchen. He said his transformation to minimalist winemaker started slowly: "I asked myself what was absolutely necessary to make wine."

He began to strip the tools and ingredients away, one by one. He found out the only thing he needed was a container to hold the grapes, his feet for stomping, and barrels to put the wine in. Along the way, he realized that he couldn't tolerate sulfur. He reduced his usage until there was sometimes none at all. "Do you know there was very little sulfur used before the '70s in Burgundy?" he asked me.

Bizot's first vintage without sulfur came in 1998. Besides the lid sulfur puts on the wine, he speculates that it also increases the extraction. "And you know that blackcurrant in Pinot?" he asked. He said that comes from mercaptan, a wine flaw usually characterized by a cabbage-like smell. And, yes, he also attributes that to the effect sulfur can have on a wine.

He raises his wines, no matter from which soils, in 100 percent new oak, a choice which scared me. His reasoning is that with new oak he can avoid sulfuring barrels before usage. My first wine of his, over that eggplant, was a 2007 Hautes-Côtes white. I found it overpowered by the vanilla of wood, but still there was an intriguing wine beneath. It was impossible to be indifferent about it.

The domaine is barely more than a postage stamp. Bizot started out with 2.5 hectares split among fragmented parcels in Vosne and Flagey-Echézeaux. He recently added an extra hectare in three parcels of old vine acquisitions: south of Dijon, Bourgogne Le Chapitre, and Marsannay Clos du Roy.

Down through a blue door, into a typical shallow ancient cellar weeping moisture, we tasted a few of his 2011s. Even in their infancy, depending on the terroir, they handled the oak differently. The Marsannay Clos du Roy, from a dry and hot terroir, had the hardest time integrating the oak. I was deeply impressed, however, by the cooler parcels. The Vosne Les Jachées (the parcel he was peeved with earlier in the evening) had such vibrancy. The Echézeaux Grand Cru was more angular.

Much is made of Bizot's having lived down the block from the late god-like winemaker Henri Jayer, a relationship that was formally deified in *The Drops of God*, a fabulous Japanese manga. It's practically apocryphal. Writers have spread it around that Jayer was Jean Yves' mentor (Robert Parker's ex-Burgundy critic, Pierre-Antoine Rovani, was responsible for much of this). I asked what the truth was. "I said to Pierre-Antoine, many years ago now, that I learned more about wine speaking with Jayer in three hours than in two years of studying enology," Bizot said. "He somehow concluded I was a disciple of Jayer. I think it's a little bit short-sighted. My home is less than 100 meters up from his house. We sometimes discussed wines."

He believes Jayer had a lot to teach him about how the job doesn't stop when the wine is made, that marketing is important. But, he continued, "Our ways to make wine are quite opposite." Consider their positions on the stems (Bizot uses 100 percent of the stems, while Jayer destemmed) or on cold maceration (Bizot uses none, while it was Jayer's calling card). "But the main lesson—and the most important—I received from him is to free myself from the common and usual rules to make wine. In his era, he imagined another solution, completely different from what other producers were doing. So, in this meaning, yes, I agree, I am a disciple of Jayer. We find our own solutions to problems."

Even with the star status bestowed on him by *The Drops of God*, Bizot doesn't get a lot of press. This might be due to his breathtaking prices. But is he an interesting man? Absolutely. Should you buy his wines, if you have the money and the curiosity? Absolutely. Anyway, I'm a sucker for 100 percent stem vinification. Remember to give it some age. Give that oak a chance to meld, and the stems to do their magic trick. You don't have to wait for your grandchildren's college graduation to open it, but ten years should pay you back royally.

Winemaker Profile: Bernard Van Berg (Côte de Beaune)

High above nowhere lies some land, not far from Meursault, where only a crazy person would plant vines. Here, that crazy person is Bernard Van Berg. His first priority was to acquire a piece of Burgundy in a rural place, in a natural place. After that he was convinced he would respect the land and the land would respect the wine.

His parents, Dutch by origin, were vacationing in France when World War II broke out. The couple managed to get to Switzerland and remained there in safety. They then moved to Brussels, where Van Berg was raised. He claims to have discovered his passion for wine when he was five years old. Left in the dinner room while the men went to smoke, he drained the wine remaining in the glasses, then went to ask his father, "Papa, why is the room spinning?" By the time he was 18, he had graduated to knocking on the door of Domaine de la Romanée-Conti (it was expensive, but at 20 euros or so at the time, not so bad). Years later, past 50 and ready to indulge a growing desire to make wine, he gave up photography and moved with his wife, Judith, to Meursault in 2001, putting out his first vintage in 2002. He then set out to find his own way of making wine, having no idea there was such a thing as natural winemaking.

When I visited, it had started to storm, and he handed me an umbrella. We drove to a corner of Meursault I never knew existed, far away from the Grands Crus. There, on two hectares of forgotten land, allocated to ordinary wine, Pinot, Gamay, Chardonnay, and Aligoté, that Van Berg has brought a sense of grace.

Van Berg has made some startling decisions, such as training some of his Chardonnay and Gamay in that bean pole trellising, échalas, as on the steep slopes of the northern Rhône, and unseen anywhere else in Burgundy.

He chose his plots far away from the intensive farming in the fancy part of Burgundy. For him, it was essential to find a rural spot filled with life and biodiversity. He purchased 4 hectares while only working 2, ensuring enough natural land to support his vision. From the very beginning, he was out to prove that there were historical plots ignored by the authorities that map the lands of Burgundy.

He believed that these neglected patches could produce spectacular wines if one used uncompromising discipline. Working on instinct, he uses organic and herbal teas for farming. Some vineyard soils are worked by horse, others plowed by hand. Some, like one plot of Chardonnay vines, have not been tilled in six years.

As an artist, it makes sense that Van Berg works on instinct. But it is rare that a vineyard is such a natural extension of a person. "Bernard won't eat meat," his wife Judith told me," because he doesn't want to kill animals, and he often escorts insects off the roads or returns frogs to the pond so they won't be killed." I could easily envision the vigneron focusing on a plant to sense what it wanted. Did it desire the bondage of cordon? Did it want the freedom and stretch of *échalas*? "The goal is that the vine, as well as the winemakers, have positive energies," Judith explained.

On that day, I was quickly starting to resemble a drowned rat, and the gentleman took pity on my soaking paws. We retreated into the shelter, and he took me on a quick walk through the cuverie. I cast about looking for clues. He uses a vertical press so tiny it is almost toy-like. He has 100 percent new wood barrels for his *élevage*. Except for an orange wine he once made, he always uses stems, whole-cluster, and foot-treading. The red wines never have sulfur, but the white wines have very small amounts. His Danish importer asked him to give up even that little bit of SO_2, but he clings to it.

When the laws changed in 2012 and Vin de France allowed the vintage to be posted on the bottle, he opted out of Bourgogne Grand Ordinaire (BGO is now obsolete, and this was replaced by the perceived more marketable Coteaux Bourguignons appellation). To make his point, he opted for Bordeaux-style bottles. After tasting the wines, I had no idea how he ever won the classification, as they could dramatically challenge the conventional notion of wine from the Côte d'Or.

Finally, we sat down to taste. The wines are delicate in every way, except the prices, which are breathtakingly expensive and a perfect counterpoint to an issue on value. After all, how could you place a value on these wines? Van Berg rarely makes more than 2,000 bottles, which sounds a lot larger than the actual 168 cases in total. Does that make him the tiniest commercial winery in Burgundy? I know for sure he's about the most eccentric.

News flash: The rare wine he makes is slated to become rarer, as bowing to the devastating frost and hail that wiped out his crop in 2016, he has made the painful decision to try to sell off most of his land to someone who will continue in his philosophy. I wish him a soulful buyer, but I mourn the loss. Burgundy needs outliers like Van Berg.

How to Not Lose Your Shirt Drinking Burgundy

In coming years, we will see a tremendous drop in Burgundy availability, as there have been an inordinate number of low and almost no-yield vintages of late, due to dramatic weather and loss from hail. This means that an expensive wine will be rarer and indeed more expensive. But that shouldn't mean you have to do without. There are a few wines that everyone seems to want, and even when Burgundy prices go nuts, some others, even great producers such as Jean-Claude Rateau, can't seem to get enough attention. So do what you'd do in the best of worlds, even if there were wines-a-plenty: Buy a great producer's cheapest wines. Look for wines in the outer boroughs. Look for brand new producers before they get too hot. Many on the list below fall into this category.

WHO TO DRINK

- Domaine Berthaut; Fixin (in conversion to organic)
- Sylvain Pataille; Marsannay (biodynamic)
- Jean-Louis Trapet; Gevrey-Chambertin (biodynamic)
- Jane et Sylvain; Gevrey-Chambertin (organic)
- Domaine Ballorin; Morey-Saint-Denis (biodynamic)
- Domaine Arlaud; Morey-Saint-Denis (biodynamic)
- Domaine de la Romanée-Conti; Vosne-Romanée (biodynamic)
- Bruno Clavelier; Vosne-Romanée (biodynamic)
- Jean-Yves Bizot; Vosne-Romanée (organic)
- Nicolas Faure; Nuits-Saint-Georges (organic)
- Domaine Prieuré-Roch; Nuits-Saint-Georges (biodynamic)
- Jacques-Frédéric Mugnier; Chambolle-Musigny (sustainable)
- Chandon-de-Briailles; Savigny-lès-Beaune (biodynamic)
- François de Nicolay; Savigny-lès-Beaune (organic)
- Maison Harbor; Savigny-lès-Beaune (organic)
- Chanterêves; Savigny-lès-Beaune (sustainable, organic)
- Domaine Simon Bize; Savigny-lès-Beaune (biodynamic)
- Emmanuel Giboulot; Beaune (biodynamic)
- Philippe Pacalet; Beaune (sustainable, organic)
- Domaine Jean-Claude Rateau; Beaune (biodynamic)
- Domaine Lafarge; Volnay (biodyanmic)
- Fanny Sabre; Pommard (organic)
- Domaine Heitz-Lochardet; Chassagne-Montrachet (biodynamic)
- Jean-Marc Roulot; Meursault (organic)

- Renaud Boyer; Meursault (organic)
- Domaine Bernard Van Berg; Meursault (organic)
- Domaine de Chassorney/Frederic Cossard; Saint-Romain (biodynamic)
- Domaine d'Auvenay; Auxey-Duresses (biodynamic)
- Domaine Dominique Derain; Saint-Aubin (biodynamic)
- Domaine Sextant/Julien Altaber; Saint-Aubin (biodynamic)
- Maison En Belles Lies/Pierre Fenals; Saint-Aubin (biodynamic)
- Domaine Hubert Lamy; Saint-Aubin (sustainable)
- Domaine des Rouges-Queues; Maranges (biodynamic)
- Domaine Chevrot; Maranges (biodynamic)
- Domaine Naudin-Ferrand; Hautes Côtes (organic, sustainable)

Burgundy Suburbs

Just as New York City isn't limited to Madison Avenue, there's a lot more to Burgundy than the Côte d'Or. Sure, those golden slopes deliver exquisite wine, but there is life and dirt elsewhere. And that's where the creative newcomers are going, as well as the outliers who always worked well.

CHABLIS: Welcome to Burgundy's equivalent of the Upper East Side. Quiet, conservative Chablis has long rested on its past reputation of producing some of the most interesting Chardonnay: stony and mineral, lean, austere, compelling, flinty. In Chablis, the climate is continental and the land is exposed, barely protected from the northern wind. This explains why the best vineyards are south west facing, in order to get the last bit of the sun's warmth to help them get to ultimate ripening.

Back in 1864, Dr. Jules Guyot described the local vintages this way: "Chablis wines have a fine gold color, with a green tint. They are strong, although not overly so, and their bouquet is charming. They are distinguished by . . . the lively, beneficial and lucid way they stimulate the mind." But in the past three decades, very few stimulated my mind, forget about the palate. Chablis went through a dark period of trying to have the richness of Meursault and of California Chardonnay. Gone was its charm. On top of that, it has become riddled with commercial plantings and commercial winemaking and commercial viticulture. The total population of organic producers in the region, for the longest time, could be balanced on the head of a pin. But that started to change with one particular couple, Alice and Olivier de Moor. I remember well when I first met them at a wine fair in France. It was in 2007, and the whole room was buzzing about the wines. Stars are born for a good reason, and in this case it was not only because they were a handsome couple. It is in their hands. I remembered the class of the wine, whether it was in their fine Aligoté or their Bel Air Chablis.

Much is made of the limestone-based soils of Chablis. You can't spend much time there before you start hearing the words Portlandian and Kimmeridgian thrown around. The Portlandian-based soils are younger and simpler and have less clay; they're basically weathered, harder limestone. They're said to make a fruitier wine, and you'll find most of the rare red wines in the region of Auxerre planted on them. Kimmeridgian marl is royalty. Its outcropping runs from Champagne to Chablis to the Loire, under the Channel, and pops up in England, where they are capitalizing on the famous limestone to make sparkling wine. It has a greater mineral-rich clay and a greater intensity of the under-sea-beastie shells the region is riddled with. Go into any tasting room or cellar and you'll see the comma-shaped, tiny *Exogyra virgula*, a type of extinct oyster, and the spiral coils of ammonites the vigneron has plucked from the earth, all proudly displayed.

It is the Kimmeridgian rock that is said to give the wines that legendary flint flavor. In fact, some say if you break off a piece of the comma-shaped fossils, the aroma is that very flint that can come in the wines. Is this just a trumped-up myth? You'll have to see for yourself, but you'll have to find a winemaker who works organically with little or no sulfur and farms on soils riddled with those shells. The names of Raveneau and Dauvissat are the blue chips in the area. But wines to drink here come from the biodynamic Alice and Olivier, as well as the developing wines of Pattes Loup, the organic and classic from Lilian and Gérard Duplessis. And there's much more to come, with Athénaïs de Béru leading the pack.

HAUTES CÔTES: This is the catchall phrase for the vineyard land above the Côte d'Or at higher elevation, with cooler and drier weather, more marl, little subsoil, and less limestone. Here, the future is looking up.

This area is like Brooklyn's Bushwick neighborhood, an industrial area that became hot because artists who moved in who needed space and affordability. Hautes Côtes used to be chock-full of chemicals and machine farming, but things are changing in this region that runs along the western edge of the Côte de Nuits and Beaune, with borders touching Nuits-Saint-Georges, Pernand-Vergelesses, Saint-Romain, and other communes. There's a lot of clay in spots and a lot of great limestone and clay mix. There are no specifically lauded vineyards. The place was never respected, and to be honest, before the advent of climate change, it was probably too cold to produce good fruit, but that has all changed in the past fifteen years.

What's more, the new folk here are deep into dirt. Here's a place for value, with plenty of Gamay and Pinot Noir and Aligoté and Chardonnay. Look for Domaines Naudin-Ferrand, Domaine Montchovet, Nicolas Faure, Fanny Sabre, and Jean-Claude Rateau.

CÔTE CHALONNAISE: This area is south of the Côte d'Or, but in fact cooler because there's less protection on the west side and the landscape is more hilly. So the wines, especially red ones, can be a bit sharper. The best vineyards are classified as Premier Cru. There are no Grand Cru.

Welcome to Burgundy's Murray Hill. It's a region that's been there forever but somehow just hasn't taken off. As soon as you leave the very last bit of the fancy Côte d'Or you hit the Côte Chalonnaise. One town is quite well known for its red, and that's Mercurey. The producers to look for there work biodynamically; consider Domaine Derain (whose winery is in Saint-Aubin) and Michel Juillot. A few minutes northwest is Bouzeron. This is the village that houses the A. & P. Villaine domaine. While their Pinot Noirs are quite lovely, they're a little more chunky than you'd find over in the Côte d'Or. What this village is truly known for is its Aligoté. Aubert de Villaine, the managing director of Burgundy's most revered house, owns the biodynamic domaine with his wife Pamela. His nephew Pierre de Benoist makes the wine and will carry it on to the next generation.

THE MÂCONNAIS: For Burgundy, this is a warmer climate, but still snuggly within the cool climate category. Unlike the core of Burgundy, they experience the "*vent du Midi*," the powerful wind that blows from the west, cold in the winter and warm in the growing season. This is especially fierce in the Monts du Mâconnais, the hills that separate the granite of the Beaujolais on the west and the slope of limestone on the east where most of the vineyards are found. It is there, under the warm summer wind that the grapes grow with greater ripeness.

While there is also silica-laced soil on granitic bedrock (around Saint-Véran), vines were first planted here on the limestone soils in Gallo-Roman times and were fostered in the Middle Ages by the powerful abbeys of Tournus and Cluny. Rural, with a great extent of biodiversity, you'll find some truly excellent Gamay here, often from old stock, as well as Aligoté and Pinot Noir. There are several names you want to make sure not to miss. Domaine des Vignes du Maynes is a spiritual and important domaine. The Bret Brothers, who make wines with bought grapes under that label as well as their own wines under the name La Soufrandière, are doing fabulous stuff. Both growers are biodynamic. Is that a coincidence? Probably not. Olivier Merlin's wines are accessible and honest. Céline and Laurent Tripoz are great, especially if you're looking for some very delicious sparkling wines. The closest thing they have down there to a cult domaine are the Valette wines. These can age with tremendous depth. Organic since 1990, Philippe Valette devotes himself to one grape, Chardonnay. Valette picks the grapes when they're super-ripe, but the alcohols remain reasonable. He ages the wines for two years in the barrel on the fine lees. The results are wines that can work just as well right out of the shop as they do twenty years later.

The Jura

Like many a forgotten region, the Jura in the Bourgogne-Franche-Comté, a 45-minute drive east of Dijon, used to be a contender. Before the scourge of phylloxera, the region had a solid reputation. They had the ultimate bragging rights: Their wines were served at court. There were about 50,000 hectares of vines in the middle of the 19th century, but by 2014, this had shrunk dramatically to about 2,200 hectares. Sequestered away, the region remained a big secret for a long time. But now, the small rural region has hipster appeal. Don't hold that against it. The Jura is a talented spot, with wines of remarkable energy and eccentricity, and other charms like morel mushrooms, Comté cheese, and Louis Pasteur's final home and laboratory. Wine is back, and it's not just for the odd experiments that result in sherry-like wines and delicate reds with wildly fascinating tastes.

In addition, for the past thirty years, the Jura has been known for being the home to its bonafide guru, Pierre Overnoy. He has, in his quiet, humble way, become an unassuming revered figure for those who search for honesty and purity in wine. Overnoy works as naturally as he can. His wines are long-lived and complex and old-fashioned in their authenticity. His ethereal cuvées have become a standard, and he's launched a generation which follows in his footsteps, even as he's stepped aside to let his chosen heir, Emmanuel Houillon, take the lead. Overnoy's legacy is located on the foothills of the Alps. While it's not completely Alpine, with all of those cows and the fresh air, it feels like it. Then again, with the influx of dreadlocks on many of the winemakers' heads, it also feels a little rock 'n' roll. Speaking of rock, there is marl with some limestone and schist. Walk in the vines, collect fossils of the delicate star-shaped pentacrines and the occasional seahorse. It's its own kind of magic.

The Dirt

The Jura department, bordered by the Saône Plain and the Jura Mountains, will always be linked to the dinosaurs as the limestone and clay marl soils date back to the Triassic and Jurassic Periods. But links to Burgundy are also often made as they are mirror images of each other, separated by the Saône.

Like nearby Burgundy, the Jura was once underwater and subject to the turmoil that would become the Alps. When the sea retreated, underwater caverns, now exposed, caved in and crumbled, resulting in rocks, sand, and silt. When the Alps were forming, the Earth slid and folded multiple times, trapping oysters, corals, star-shaped pentacrines, and all manner of sea creatures that don't show up in Burgundy that often.

The resulting Jura soil, so fine for grape growing, is a stratum of marl limestone and schists, metamorphic and sedimentary. And it is also differentiated from Burgundy by being nestled into the undulating mountain foothills with a more extreme climate.

Opinions on where to plant which vine verge on religious doctrine. One winter, Pascaline and I were visiting Julien Labet in Rotalier, down in the south of the Jura. Labet is just around the corner from superstar winemaker Jean-François (Fanfan) Ganevat. In Labet's cellar, there was a library of rocks in all sorts of colors: blues, terracottas, whites, yellows. He has an astounding 32 different cuvées, and with each one we were treated to a lecture on the wide spectrum of rocks in the region: blue and gray marls, some flat, some iridescent; rust-colored shaley marl; fossil-laden limestone. But the main issue here is the level of water retention and, of course, drainage, as the Jura tends to be wet. Labet picked up a slab of a rock he said was from the end of the Jurrasic Period—lias: a blue-gray clay rock of lime and sandstone. "This lias is the soil for Chardonnay. You can see it struggle." I put it to my nose. It had the oddest smell, like patchouli.

The Grapes

After the Jura was devastated by phylloxera, its vines were grafted onto the curative American rootstock, but only the top five most popular varieties—out of scores—were replanted. Chardonnay was one of the lucky ones. Today, it makes up 42 percent of the white varieties in the Jura which, as much as I like its expression here, seems like too much in a land where there are deserving indigenous vines. It is planted as a filler where other grapes seem sad. You'll see it mixed with Savagnin or in wonderful bubbly wines made in the style of Champagne, called Crémant du Jura. Melon Queue Rouge is a rare variation of Chardonnay. Think of it as a Chardonnay with a red tail (hence the "queue" in the name). It's kind of delicious, and Philippe Bornard, Jean-François Ganevat, and Domaine de la Pinte make ones worth seeking out. The second most planted white grape is Savagnin. This is important here, and is very particular. Its old name is Naturé, also known as Traminer. It is early-budding, early-ripening, and thick-skinned. It's known to be the parent grape of Savagnin, Chenin Blanc, and also Grüner Veltliner. But unlike its children, this grape stayed at home. Barely anyone grows it outside of the Jura, aside from a few small plantings in Austria, Germany, and Italy. It grows best on the slopes of blue-gray marls, which soften its often strange and piercing acidity.

Pinot Noir is also here. In the past, this was plunked into field blends. But with Burgundy 45 minutes away, it is of course reasonable that they would be bottled all by themselves. Like all wines from this area, it's best without extraction. It is said to do best in the south on the Bajocian (middle Jurrasic) limestone, or wherever the drainage is good, such as on gravelly soils.

Poulsard (in the tiny town of Pupillin, it's called Ploussard), is a Jura original and makes up about 14 percent of all plantings. Early-ripening and early-budding, it loves marl soils, especially the reddish ones, which keep the earth's warmth. It has a fruit-tea-like look and its taste can be whispery. You'll hear it often said that wherever Savagnin is happy, so is Poulsard, like Jack and Jill. But then, Poulsard is rather difficult and finicky, though much adored. Overall, it's a thin-skinned grape that delivers a pale, translucent, pleasing wine with a depth that defies its color.

Trousseau, another grape associated with the Jura, is the Bastardo of Spain. Early-ripening and early-budding, it needs time. And like a cat in the sun, it loves the heat—which it doesn't get that much of in this sub-Alpine region—and craves gravel and clay. It is prone to some reduction, and some of its aromas can seem a little sulfury, but don't worry; just pour it into a wide-mouthed pitcher or decanter. Currently, the grape is enjoying new plantings in California and has a sexy aura; it's the anti-Merlot.

Like everyone else, the first time I ordered a Savagnin from the Jura, I thought it was a Sauvignon. The idiot sommelier didn't warn me, and I was too timid to ask what strange beast was in my glass. It was a wine that tasted just like sherry. I loved it, but was confused. Here's what was going on. The most distinctive wines from the region are made from Savagnin, in either a straight-forward kind of vinification known as *ouillé*, or in Vin Jaune, which is what I had ordered, a *non-ouillé*. *Ouillé* means "topped off," so *non-ouillé* means that the wine was not covered to keep it protected from oxygen while in the barrel. When wine isn't protected, a *voile* (which translates into "veil") of yeast forms on the surface of the wine. This is almost identical to the *flor* of Jerez, or Sherry *flor* yeast and acts the same way. It protects the wine from turning into vinegar, but it also transforms fruitiness into nuttiness and savory flavors, concentrating these until bottling. Some of the aromas and tastes include curry, Band-Aids and high-toned shoe polish. While more simple, younger wines can be made in a *non-ouillé* fashion, the best wines are often selected to become a Vin Jaune, which must age in a barrel until the December six years after harvest. They're then bottled into a *clavelin*, a squat bottle of 62 centiliters, just shy of the normal 750ml wine bottle. The difference is said to represent the amount lost to the aging process, also known as the angels' share. There is one appellation devoted entirely to Vin Jaune: Château-Chalon. Historically, the Vins Jaunes are released during the first weekend of the February bacchanal la Percée du Vin Jaune.

Winemaker Profile: Pierre Overnoy

It was a white winter when a little train of pilgrims and I were banging the snow off our boots, waiting for Pierre Overnoy to open his door. Grinning, he accepted the shower of hello kisses from those of us he knew, shook hands with those of us he did not, then ushered us beyond his humble kitchen into the back receiving room.

Overnoy, stooped, is nearing 80, but is world-famous for his soul, his wines, and his bread. He is also an unlikely rock star. With 622 Instagram mentions (last I looked), he's segued from obscure to absolute. People buy the wines just because they can—for status, not pleasure. This means those of us who worship the Poulsard and the Savagnins can rarely afford or even find them in countries like the United States or France. (There's better hunting in Japan, Georgia, the UK, and even Germany.)

This vigneron was born, raised, and formed in rural and peaceful Pupillin, in the north of the Jura, a few kilometers outside of

Arbois. He is known as the Pope of Pupillin, but even though he is a devout Catholic, think of him more as Pupillin's Dalai Lama.

The domaine was established in 1968, and designated scion Emmanuel came on in 2001. They make a superb Chardonnay, a Savagnin that is sometimes *ouillé* and sometimes not, a blend of Chardonnay, and Savagnin, a long-aged Ploussard (as they call the Poulsard in this village), and, rarely, Vin Jaune. Because there's no grape name on the label it might be difficult to know what's inside, unless you know the code. The secret is in the color of wax on the capsule: White is chardonnay. Yellow is Savagnin. Grey is the Chardonnay and Savagnin blend. And the Clavelin bottle tells you it's the Vin Jaune.

The area's first organic vineyard, as well as the first committed to all-natural methods, Overnoy has inspired ethereal wines all over the Jura, such as Domaine des Miroirs, who take Overnoy's philosophy to its extreme, drawing the thinnest line between wine and cloud.

Overnoy never starts a tasting without genuinely asking about his guests, and he does not neglect the newcomers. Then he almost always starts by talking about his long-dead guru, Jules Chauvet, considered the father of the natural wine movement.

"Chauvet said 'make wine low in alcohol, and keep CO_2 in the wine,'" Overnoy recalled.

But the real secret, he said, is the work in the vineyard to achieve balance in the vine. The wines of Domaine Overnoy-Houillon almost always have a slight fizz to start and are low in alcohol. The first wine we tasted was the 2011 Savagnin, an exquisite example of the philosophy of balance. Bottled September 4, 2014, it was limpid, with a touch of caramel, and it was deep, very deep, complex and delicious. It was young at first, then floral, with a great big lemon-like acidity that was simply stunning. The 2012 Ploussard, with its blood-orange color, had a spine that went straight up and down and had the flexibility of a dancer. Bottled September 5, 2013, it was a little cold, and Overnoy snuggled the glass under his sweater, caressing the bowl, coaxing it to warm up. "Ploussard is as fragile as crystal," he said. Then he confessed that in 2014, they lost 80 percent of their Ploussard due to a fly, the suzukii. A vinegar fly, it preys on whole young fruit and pretty much decimated the red grapes of the area.

Then it was blind tasting time. An aged wine arrived. "With a very old wine," Overnoy advised, "you have a second to take the first smell before it changes." While the wine wasn't so ancient, it was old. Its funky nose had aromas that changed with the air, plus there were some flavors of cherry and clay, so we knew it was a warm year. It was dusty, and the color was deep and garnet. It was a 1986 Ploussard made without sulfur addition.

"It wasn't as good a year as 1985," he said, "but I was better, so I made a better wine."

The wine grew shockingly young and was a revelation to one in our group, who had been unconvinced by the longevity of wines without sulfur.

Overnoy left for the kitchen. Enough with wine. We were to get rewarded with bread. He emerged with a loaf wrapped in a blanket and gave us pieces, just as my grandfather used to hand out the afikomen at the Passover seder.

We dived more into conversation. His favorite wine to drink, it turns out, is the 1945 Figeac Bordeaux. As we looked around at all of the books in the room, Pascaline asked what he liked to read.

Pierre grew a little apologetic. "I never learned to read well," he said quietly. The story is that he hated school and preferred to spend time in the vines and in the forest, hunting. Here was a paradox: He is such a learned man, but isolated from the joy and study of books. We kept on tasting and talking and tasting.

Eventually, I asked Overnoy how he felt about the ballooning prices of his wines, especially in Paris and in New York.

"The wines are between 14 to 18 euros from my door," he said. Overnoy added that he wouldn't raise his prices, but it pained him to see his bottles go for so much more money elsewhere. In Paris you can't find them, and in New York, the wholesale price is about $30. If you find it on a restaurant's wine list you're likely to see it at mark up of at least 400%—and that's for a new vintage. It is one of the most highly coveted wines in the city. This is an uncomfortable reality for him, yet he won't buy grapes and become a *négociant*, as some others, most notably Jean-François Ganevat, has done, because he fears his quality would suffer. "The very disturbing problem is, I don't want my wine to be for rich people. Remember," Pierre said, "wine is first a beverage for drinkability."

And there with the bread in his hand, in a home with none of the riches that his wines bring others, we contemplated the man and the magic, then ganged up on him for group photos.

WHO TO DRINK

- Domaine Désiré Petit; Pupillin (biodynamic)
- Domaine de la Pinte; Pupillin (biodynamic)
- Philippe et Tony Bornard; Pupillin (organic)
- Domaine Pierre Overnoy and Emmanuel Houillon; Pupillin (biodynamic)
- Renaud Bruyère-Adeline Houillon; Pupillin (biodynamic)
- Michel Gahier; Arbois (organic)

- Domaine de l'Octavin; Arbois (biodynamic)
- Stéphane Tissot; Arbois (biodynamic)
- Domane de Saint-Pierre; Arbois, Côtes du Jura (organic)
- Domaine de la Loue; Arbois (organic)
- Domaine des Bodines; Arbois (organic)
- Domaine de la Tournelle; Arbois (organic)
- Domaine des Cavarodes; Côtes du Jura (organic)
- Domaine des Marnes Blanches; Côtes du Jura (organic)
- Didier Grappe; Côtes du Jura (organic)
- Domaine des Miroirs; Côtes du Jura (organic)
- Peggy et Jean-Pascal Buronfosse; Rotalier, Côtes du Jura (organic)
- Jean-Francois Ganevat; Rotalier, Côtes du Jura (organic)
- Julien Labet, Rotalier; Côtes du Jura (organic)

Champagne

"The coldest winter I ever spent was summer in San Francisco," is often attributed (incorrectly, it turns out) to Mark Twain. Well, whoever said it, it's probably safe to say that he or she never visited Champagne. On my first serious visit, in the summer, it snowed in the vineyards. I was dead sick the next day. Whether January or July, snow is likely here. That, in conjunction with soils so poor they are the poster child for making lemonade when life hands you lemons. But that bereft soil, so poor and unfertile? It turns out that white chalk soil, with little serious clay, in combination with place, is part of the sorcery that created Champagne.

Like most other places in France, in Champagne the first grapes were planted by the Romans. Further down the road, wine became important because Reims was coronation central, and all of those kings and queens needed something to anoint the process. The wines had a reputation, but they sure weren't Burgundy. This area was tough. This was no place to ripen red grapes, except in certain unexpectedly hot years, and in certain places where there was more clay. But they grew red grapes here anyway. The wines were anemic and so high in acid, it set drinkers' tooth enamel to screaming. But then, through either some freak accident or keen observations, there came the bubbles (from a restart of fermentation). From there, they learned to corral the fizz—though this didn't truly happen until the 1800s with the advent of sturdier bottles from England. And then the world rejoiced.

The Dirt

The chalk here is the same stuff found on blackboards and in sidewalk art, and early cosmetic and face powder. Chalk is commonly thought of as a texture as well as a soil, but in fact, it is a specific type of sedimentary rock. Cognac and Jerez (what we know as Sherry) have it, but their climates are very different. Both have strong Atlantic sea influences; brilliant sun and heat for Jerez, a bit milder for Cognac. No: A land of chalk and Champagne is a totally different animal. Historically, it's about grapes that just barely ripened.

Champagne's soils are full of limestone, of course, but it is the highly soft and porous chalk that people say makes the difference—and why it is like no other sparkling wine.

Chalk is the softer, more porous limestone, almost solely composed of calcium carbonate with the tiniest bit of clay. There are two kinds of chalk in Champagne. The one nearest the surface is quite hard. This is called belemnite, and it is formed from cuttlefish skeletons. It's from the Tertiary Period, after mammals replaced dinosaurs. The second type of chalk is the micraster, from sea urchin and starfish fossils, dating back to when the dinosaurs still roamed.

The beauty of the chalk is its ability to drain. And in a wet clime like Champagne, it is what makes or breaks the vines. Up north, plots of land in Grands and Premiers Crus are celebrated but is it really the only soil that delivers? Try going down south to the area of the Aube, near the lovely medieval city of Troyes. This is a region that has been abused and insulted for its lack of soil grandeur. Now, it's a home for fabulously inventive winemakers and as it is slightly warmer, they plant more red grapes, Pinot Noir and Pinot Meunier, and make floral Champagnes from them. There, the soil is mostly similar to that of Chablis, developed on older Kimmeridgian marls—a clay and limestone mix. But there is indeed one chalky hill, almost like the chalk's last gasp, in the region of Montgueux, where the grape of choice is Chardonnay.

But no matter how good your soil is, it can be pretty bad if you don't farm well and pick for quality instead of volume. Champagne has been long known as the land of brands more than for vineyards and good farming. We know the big names. They rarely own land, but have contracts with farmers all over. They also control the farming. Industrial methods came in strong in the 1970s, and soon most of Champagne fell into cynical winemaking of sugar and bubbles. But that started to change as more individual landowners, instead of selling all of their grapes to the big houses like Moët & Chandon and Clicquot, started to farm for their own wine. This revolution in "grower Champagne" started in the late '70s and has finally blossomed into a glorious resurrection of the soul of Champagne.

The most famous land is in the northeast, a mere 45 minutes from Paris by train, the Vallée de la Marne. This is mostly where they add Pinot Meunier to the blend. To its east is the Montagne de Reims, which is mostly Pinot Noir land. Côte des Blancs is Chardonnay on mostly chalk-based soils. Going south, a region that is so up-and-coming we can't keep track, is the previously-mentioned Aube, with mostly black grapes and the rarely mentioned (for now) Côte de Sézanne. Unlike other regions, Champagne has villages that are rated instead of vineyards; there are 17 Grand Cru villages and 43 Premier Cru villages. All of the Grands Crus are in the Marne, but Montgueux is also considered to be at the top level, even if it doesn't carry the designation.

MONTAGNE DE REIMS

- Sillery
- Puisieulx
- Beaumont-sur-Vesle
- Verzenay
- Mailly-Champagne
- Verzy
- Louvois
- Bouzy
- Ambonnay

VALLÉE DE LA MARNE

- Aÿ
- Tours-sur-Marne

CÔTE DE BLANCS

- Chouilly
- Oiry
- Cramant
- Avize
- Oger
- Le Mesnil-sur-Oger

What is Méthode Champenoise?

There is only one true Champagne, and it's made in Champagne. But the method is used worldwide. Outside of the original region, they must be called sparkling wines, or *vin mousseux*, or *spumante* (in Italy).

But there are regional names as well. In France, there are eight regions that use the name crémant. Cava is the regional name used in the Penedès in Spain. Franciacorta, also in Italy, is their DOCG devoted to sparkling wine made with this method. The process for the method goes like this: Start with still wine. Bottle it. Restart fermentation by introducing yeast, more sugar, or sweet wine—the latter, if you want to do as the natural folk do. The refermentation produces carbon dioxide and alcohol. The CO_2 is trapped in the bottle, and pressure builds up. When the wine has spent enough time on the lees (as the yeasts die after this second fermentation in the bottle), that deposit is disgorged (basically, it's a plug of gunk that is removed.)

Then there are variations on that theme regarding sweetness level, called dosage (which refers to sugar added to the wine to adjust sweetness, after disgorgement and before bottling). As climate change has encroached and farming practices have improved, Champagne is being made with riper and riper grapes. As a result, there is a proliferation of wines made with no dosage. There you go: Champagne. In the end, while bubbly wines are made all over the world, no other kind comes close. Even with the bad producers—and God knows there's a lot of really lousy, overly sweet, commercial plonk in Champagne—somehow it all tastes like Champagne.

The Grapes

You'll see Blanc de Blancs on a label of Champagne. This means it is made from white grapes. Blanc de Noirs is a white champagne made from red grapes.

There are a few rare old white grapes, like Arbane, Petit Meslier, and more well known varieties like Pinot Gris and Pinot Blanc, but Champagne is mostly led by a trio of grapes, two of which are very familiar.

The white Chardonnay and the red Pinot Noir are widely grown around the world in all sorts of soils. But Pinot Meunier, an increased darling of the area, has not ventured out much. A mutation of Pinot, it has a downy leaf and is relatively hearty. The traditional blend is a third of each grape, and it is said that the Meunier gives the fruit, the Pinot Noir gives the richness, and the Chardonnay gives the finesse. But don't worry if it doesn't seem that way to you.

The wines are labeled by their sweetness, depending on how high the dosage is. They proceed from Brut Nature (or Non-Dosage) to Extra Brut, then Brut to Extra-Dry, Dry, Demi-Sec, and Doux.

Winemaker Profile: Francis Boulard

I popped my first Boulard in 2009 under the label Raymond Boulard. I chose it because I needed a rosé and the price, at $33, was right. I had no expectations. The label was lackluster. However, the fizz inside was hardly common. It seemed to be relatively low in sulfur with a lovely, crazy wildness. This Boulard, it seemed, was a prince in pauper's clothing. Over time, those of us who were keen on the Boulards picked over the remaining bottles we could find. But eventually the beautiful Champagnes with the dull labels and cheap-looking bottles ran out. A few years later, a new white label burst on the scene: Francis Boulard & Fille. The "fille" would be his daughter, Delphine.

Escaping treacherous roads, Pascaline and I took a seat at a round table as the snow fell heavily outside, Boulard disappeared to pull bottles for us. He knew we were rushing this visit, and to be considerate, he poured fast. And as the snow piled up outside, he told his story.

Boulard started to work with his father in 1973, and his brother and sister soon joined. Somewhere around 1996, he found himself increasingly disturbed. "I always loved nature and the soil," he told us. He noticed allergic reactions to the products used in the vineyard. He noted a chemical residue in the wines. Boulard refers to himself as a 'peasant' and because of this, he had assumed that the chemicals would just disappear. They did not. When he realized this, he said he knew he had to change the way he worked.

He started to go back to the ways he had learned from his grandfather, like working with the moon and working with cover crops. Another thing on his mind was reducing the copper and sulfur used so often in the vineyard to combat the wet and mildew-prone climate. Michel Gendrier from Domaine des Huards in Cheverny was the first to tell him about biodynamics as a way to reduce these and other chemicals in the soils.

Boulard started converting half of his family's Les Rachais vineyard in 2001. It was an experiment, and he loved the results. He then proposed converting the whole estate to biodynamics. His siblings suggested a single hectare, reluctant to take on the extra work and perhaps risk. Champagne's cold and wet weather is ripe for breeding disease that's more simply dealt with by using chemicals. "They didn't get it," he said. So he took the 3 hectares of vines he was legally entitled to and officially separated from his siblings.

These kinds of family separations—feuds over how to farm, and the fear the older generations had that the young ones would destroy everything by disturbing the status quo of chemical farming—are a common Champagne story. Boulard's father was dead at the time of split, so his troubles were with his siblings. Other younger pups (Cédric Bouchard in Celles-sur-Ource, for example) have to deal with disgruntled fathers, even though their work is wildly sought after. As a result of having gone through family strife and survived,

Boulard is sometimes pressed into an avuncular mediating role, helping the younger generation carve their own path by returning to nature. He spoke of a time when one young producer's mother called him: "Quick, come here, Francis. They're killing each other!"

We traipsed out into the snow for a visit to the rustic, simple winery attached to Boulard's house. He vinifies in stainless steel and raises the wine in barrels of varying sizes. He employs low sulfur and a natural first fermentation. The base wines always go through malolactic fermentation, which rounds out the acids. What I love about them is that they are not perfect, but they are exciting and, like Boulard, youthful in spirit.

WHO TO DRINK

MONTAGNE DE REIMS
- Francis Boulard & Fille (biodynamic)
- Thomas Perseval (organic)
- Jérôme Prévost (organic)
- Lelarge-Pugeot (organic)
- Champagne Bérêche (organic)
- Emmanuel Brochet (organic)
- Chartogne-Taillet (organic)
- Champagne Marie-Noelle Ledru (sustainable)
- Mouzon-Leroux (organic)
- Champagne Marguet (biodynamic)
- Champagne Beaufort (aromatherapy)
- Champagne Pouillon (organic)
- Eric Rodez (organic)
- Benoit Lahaye (biodynamic)

- David Léclapart (biodynamic)

VALLÉE DE LA MARNE
- Champagne Françoise Bedel (biodynamic)
- Franck Pascal (biodynamic, energy therapy)
- Champagne Tarlant (organic)
- Georges Laval (organic, biodynamic prep)
- Laherte Frères (organic)

CÔTE DES BLANCS
- Aurélien Suenen (sustainable)
- Jacques Selosse (organic, non-certified)
- Pascal Agrapart (organic)
- Larmandier-Bernier (biodynamic)
- Pascal Doquet (organic)
- Michel Fallon (organic, non-certified)

SÉZANNE/MONTGUEUX
- Champagne Ulysse Collin (sustainable)
- Emmanuel Lassaigne (organic)

CÔTE DES BAR/LES RICEYS
- Cédric Bouchard/Roses de Jeanne (organic)
- Marie-Courtin (biodynamic)
- Roland Piollot (organic)
- Bertrand Gautherot/Vouette et Sorbée (biodynamic)
- Champagne Fleury (biodynamic)
- Val' Frison (organic)
- Charles Dufour (biodynamic)
- Ruppert-Leroy (organic)
- Olivier Horiot (biodynamic)

The Loire: Touraine

I had been drinking wine seriously for two decades when I really discovered the center cut of the Loire, the Touraine. There was one wine in particular that took me on a very different drinking path. It seemed to me to be like violet juice sipped through a chalk straw. That wine led me into the vines, embarking on a search into real wine that will never end.

I first visited the area on my bike, getting off at the Blois train station to start the adventure. It was at a time when I still believed there was no more to the Loire than Sancerre, and I had no idea there was such a thing as a Touraine. But even though I was ignorant, it was there. The Touraine is the greater appellation encompassing many smaller, intense ones. It starts as soon as you get off at that train station and stretches as far west as the town of Chinon. The land has a local kind of limestone called tuffeau (a chalky, fine-grained micaneous limestone), sand, clay, and here and there, flint. The land is profound and varied, but if you left it up to the appellation officers, they'd have you believe it's only good for insipid rosé, affordable New Zealand-like Sauvignon Blanc, wishy-washy reds, and uninspiring bubbles sold as Crémant de Loire. Talk about selling a glorious region out. Thank goodness for the fierce clutch of winemakers who cling to the glory of their land and make the wines that they do. This is a hotbed of natural winemaking and organic and biodynamic viticulture. They are in constant battle with the authorities who tell them their wines don't taste like they should, even if their lively flavors and independence resonate with drinkers worldwide. The whole Loire is one of our favorite wine areas in the world, but the Touraine, with its basket of goodies, packs in incredible diversity and value.

The Dirt

The section of the Loire Valley which lies on the way to the Atlantic Ocean, but not as far out as the Muscadet, is in the middle of château country, where the pre-revolutionary aristocracy used to play. Nowadays, it is the most glorious slice of land for wine drinkers. Its character was all set into place around 100 million to 65 million years ago during the Upper Cretaceous Period. That's when much of the Loire Valley was under the ancient seas of the Paris Basin. It was in this Turonian Stage when the compressed fragments of floating organisms and crusty sea creatures started their decomposition into the chalk layers of the Middle Loire that would later emerge as tuffeau, a gray or yellow soft and chalky limestone with a mix of mica and sand. When exposed to air, the deposits were hardened with the help of iron and magnesium oxides. When mixed with sand and flinty clays from later eras, here exist some remarkable vineyard soils.

Considered Paris's breadbasket, the region gives itself over to both thirst-quenching wines and serious ones, versatile in style and in grape. The best terroirs that give agreeable wines are almost directly on the tuffeau, on the slope of the gentle hills overlooking the Loire and its multiple tributaries. The *vin de soif*, meaning easy to drink wines, come from the flatter lands and gravelly, alluvial riverbeds.

The most well-known of the individual AOPs in the area are Chinon and Vouvray, but one should not forget Chinon's neighbor, Bourgeuil. And next to Vouvray is the rising star of Montlouis-sur-Loire, where the tuffeau gets a twist with more clay, flint, and sand.

The Grapes

The Touraine is the meeting place between the western Loire with its Chenin and Cabernet Franc, and the eastern Loire with its Sauvignon Blanc, Pinot Noir, Gamay, and Côt. There's a cornucopia of grapes with so much diversity that if you had to live your life with one appellation, you could do no better.

Côt is the local name for Malbec. Somehow it is Argentina that has transformed Malbec into the fruit bomb that has made it a household name. But going back to its origins, Malbec first showed up in Cahors, in the southwest of France. It then appeared in Bordeaux and traveled slightly north to the Loire, where I love it the best. In the Loire, Malbec is velvet, violet, and spice. The first time I had Pineau d'Aunis I put my nose in it and exclaimed that it was like Red Zinger tea! No relation to Pinot Noir or Chenin (even if Pineau d'Aunis is sometimes called Chenin Noir), there's very little of it, and too much of it is made as a rosé instead of the white peppery, fruity, velvet wine it can be. It only gets a right to an official appellation status in the Coteaux-du-Loir and Coteaux-du-Vendômois appellations, where it's most densely planted. Grolleau is even more disrespected. It pops up here, as well as in the Anjou Noir (see page 191) and is often slandered as being weedy. However, look for makers like Quentin Bourse or Marie Thibault from the town of Azay-le-Rideau. Another favorite that is on the decline and needs to be brought back with respect are the Romorantin high-acid grapes (look for it in Cour-Cheverny). Likewise, Menu Pineau is an old grape on the verge of extinction that used to be an important one in the Touraine. These rules make me so mad. Our friend Thierry Puzelat, located right outside of Blois in a town called Les Montils, used to bottle this friendly and unusual white grape as a Touraine Brin de Chèvre. As of 2016, he had to drop the Touraine and label it as a placeless Vin de France. Now he uses these grapes for the wines he raises in Georgian *quevri*.

I can see the region outlawing a grape like Viognier that doesn't belong there, but a grape that is historic to the area? Loire bureaucratic dunces!

WHO TO DRINK

- Clos du Tue Boeuf/Puzelat Brothers (organic)
- Laurent Saillard (organic)
- Pierre-Olivier Bonhomme (organic)
- Nathalie Gaubicher/Nana Vins & Co. (organic)
- Les Maisons Brûlées (organic)
- Olivier Lemasson/Les Vin Contés (organic)
- Christian Venier (organic, biodynamic)

- Noëlla Morantin (organic)
- Grégory Leclerc/Chahut et Prodiges (organic)
- Les Capriades (organic)
- Jeremy Quastana (organic)
- Julien Pineau (organic)
- Quentin Bourse/Le Sot de L'Ange; Azay-le-Rideau (organic)
- Château de la Roche; Azay-le-Rideau (organic)
- Marie Thibault; Azay-le-Rideau (organic)
- Domaine de la Garrelière/François Plouzeau (organic)
- Mikaël Bouges (organic)
- Bruno Allion (biodynamic)
- Hervé Villemade; Cheverny, Cour-Cheverny (organic)
- François Cazin; Cheverny, Cour-Cheverny (sustainable)

Vouvray and Montlouis-sur-Loire

In the very heart of this large region of Touraine, in a quiet landscape of large plateaus, fairy-tale-like valleys and white cliffs drilled with hobbit-like caves, lie two kingdoms for Chenin Blanc. On the right bank of the Loire is the larger of the two, and the most famed. This is Vouvray. Cheered by Balzac, this is the cradle of mythical sweet golden wines in the Moelleux category.

On the left bank is Montlouis-sur-Loire, for ages living in the shadow of her big sister. However, right now it's the wallflower's moment; Montlouis is at the forefront of the avant-garde natural revolution of farming and winemaking.

The gentle hills of Montlouis and Vouvray sport a trio of identical soils: gravels, tuffeau, and clay-silex—but the difference is in the details. Montlouis winemaker Damien Delecheneau of La Grange Tiphaine explained to me: "In Vouvray, you have more 'argilo-calcaire' (aubuis = clay-limestone) but also some 'argilo-silex' (perruches = clay-flint). The soils there are pretty rich, so you can go to a higher yield without losing quality. In Montlouis, you have more of the sand and silex, and poorer soils, which means lower yields." In François Pinon's words, that soil gives Vouvray more power and finesse.

Vouvray also hosts favorable conditions to develop the noble rot *Botrytis cinera* (the same rot that creates Sauternes). The *Botrytis* shrivels the grape and condenses the sugar. Thus, Vouvray produces a greater range of sweet wine. Montlouis, on the other hand, makes a greater quantity of dry wines and even has red grapes, though those are not allowed under the AOP of Montlouis-sur-Loire. But in both areas, sparkling wine is very important.

Like Sancerre in the west, Vouvray never had to try too hard because they could just sit there and be famous, so they easily fell into chemical and machine farming. There are some notable exceptions, like Domaine Huet, Philippe Foreau, and the aforementioned François Pinon, who are heroes for sure. But the failure of Vouvray gave the Montlouis star a chance to shine.

As land has been cheaper in Montlouis, it's been easier for the new committed artisans to take over land and practice their revolutionary techniques. Two of them, François Chidaine and Jacky Blot, used their influence to get some serious work done. Showing tremendous organization, they even passed through a sparkling wine called "Pétillant Originel," the first recognized AOC Pét'Nat (see sidebar). A whopping 40 percent of the AOP was either organically or biodynamically farmed in 2016, and as a result, their more famous sister, Vouvray, is finally starting to follow.

What's a Pét'Nat?

While the Loire has become famous for starting the Pét'Nat craze, really it is nothing more than a revival of an ancient way of making sparkling wine that probably first happened by accident. This is the way old prosecco was made; the process is also called *il metodo ancestrale* or *méthode ancestrale*. The wine goes into the bottle with a little unfermented sugar and the fermentation continues. The CO_2 is trapped. The result is a bubbly pleasure that is a tiny bit more grapey than the products of its more fancy cousin, the Champenoise method.

Back in the '90s, a much loved winemaker, the late Christian Chaussard, made a still wine that turned out bubbly. "Merde," he thought, "there goes that batch of wine." Turns out it was a particularly fun sparkler and even though, as Pascaline recalls, the late Gaston Huët claims the term "pétillant" was already used, the new generation shortened it to "Pét'Nat." The informal bubble spread around the world, even to Australia and the United States. It's a less expensive process than Champagne and easy to drink. The new laws in Montlouis pay it homage. It is the only standard on record where the wine must undergo natural fermentation. It also has to be on the lees for nine months, after which (unfortunately, for many who don't believe in it) the lees need to be disgorged so it is nice and clean to the eye.

WHO TO DRINK

VOUVRAY

- Domaine Huët (biodynamic)
- Clos Naudin/Philippe Foreau (sustainable)
- François Pinon (organic)
- Domaine Vincent Carême (organic)
- Michel Autran (organic)

- Mathieu Cosme (organic)
- Florent Cosme (organic)
- Sébastien Brunet (organic)
- Catherine & Pierre Breton (biodynamic)

MONTLOUIS-SUR-LOIRE

- François Chidaine (biodynamic)
- Coralie & Damien Delecheneau/La Grange Tiphaine (organic)
- Lise & Bertrand Jousset (organic)
- Frantz Saumon (organic)
- Xavier Weisskopf/Le Rocher des Violettes (organic)
- Ludovic Chanson (organic)

Chinon, Bourgueil, and Saint-Nicolas-de-Bourgueil

At the most western part of the Touraine is a trio of towns synonymous with the grape Cabernet Franc. All are worthy companions to the grape. At the top of the group, however is Chinon. It should be famous but somehow it is still not a household name.

A quote I found in a 1940s wine book, *Year Book of French Quality Wines, Spirits, & Liquors*, though not attributed to any author, might explain why Chinon, the region's largest red wine appellation of the three—therefore the one you would think would be the most popular—is still a hard sell. "It is not full of tannin like the Bordeaux, nor is it deliciously toxic like the Burgundy," the anonymous reviewer says. "It is a wine for intellectuals."

Evidently, that was written in a time when being called an intellectual was not the slur it is today. Pascaline and I drink the wines from all three appellations, so sure, go ahead and call us names.

The Dirt

While the three towns of the Touraine share similar soils and climate—wet and mild near the Atlantic, moderate by the rivers—they have distinct identities. While only minutes away from each other, the closer inland they are, the less influenced they are by the winds and the humidity from the Atlantic Ocean, with Chinon being the warmest.

Chinon lies on the Vienne River. A nuclear power plant overlooks its most famous vineyard, Les Picasses. It is the most southeast of the three, located on the left bank of the Loire. As with the other two appellations, the wines from the tuffeau slopes are profound, while the ones on the cooler, alluvial flat are simpler. The wine gets aged in wood for a year or longer when raised in the limestone, and just gets a quick fermentation and *élevage* when coming from the sand. Their rare plantings of Chenin are worth the hunt. The local rosés can be perfect and edgy spring-summer companions.

To the north on the Loire sit the other two jewels of the Touraine. Bourgueil, like Chinon, grows the best wines in the mid-slopes, and they are said to have more of a rustic edge with coarser tannins. Just try those from Pierre Breton and Domaine de la Chevalerie and be prepared to have your mind blown. Here, as in Chinon, the wines benefit from longer aging in wood. Saint-Nicolas is flatter and there's more alluvial sand and less limestone. There, the grape will give a lighter, easy-to-drink red that producers do best vinifying simply, though there are exceptions to the rule.

The Grapes

Cabernet Franc on the right soils retain acidity and show gentle fruit, yet this grape is prone to some vegetal flavor, most prominently of green bell pepper if the grapes don't get to full ripeness. But when it blends its raspberry perfume with herbal aromas, it makes for a heady, seductive philosophical conversation in a glass. Cabernet Franc loves tuffeau mixed with a little sand and clay because of its ability to clutch onto water and give the grape a drink when needed.

WHO TO DRINK

CHINON
- Domaine Baudry (organic)
- Catherine et Pierre Breton (biodynamic)
- Pascal Lambert (biodynamic)
- Olga Raffault (conversion to organic)
- Patrick Corbineau (organic)
- Château de Coulaine (organic)
- Domaine de l'R (organic)
- Caves Les Roches/Jérôme Lenoir (organic)
- Gérald Marula (organic)
- Nicolas Grobois (biodynamic)

BOURGUEIL
- Domaine de la Chevalerie (biodynamic)
- Catherine et Pierre Breton (biodynamic)
- Domaine du Mortier (organic)
- Pierre Borel (organic)
- Domaine Stéphane Guion (organic)
- Laurent Herlin (biodynamic)
- Domaine de l'Oubliée (organic)
- Aurélien Revillot (biodynamic)
- Domaine des Ouches (sustainable)

SAINT-NICOLAS-DE-BOURGUEIL
- Yannick Amirault (organic)
- Domaine du Mortier (organic)
- Sébastien David (biodynamic)

Anjou Blanc

Just next door to Bourgueil are glorious red wine zones that have gone missing. Anjou Blanc's Saumur-Champigny, for example, received appellation status for whites and reds only in 1957. Cabernet Sauvignon and Pineau d'Aunis are allowed in the AOP, but as limestone is friendly to Cabernet Franc, there are many fine domaines producing it in a single varietal—*mono-cépage*. But despite some classy wines, such as Clos Rougeard—a veritable cult Cabernet Franc—the area maintains a down-market reputation for mindless, chillable reds. That notoriety is infuriating to those who collect the wines.

The Dirt

This region is split into schist and limestone-derived soils. That's the reason they are often referred to as black and white, respectively. For this conversation, proceed directly to the metamorphic section (page 189). But meanwhile, for the Anjou regions on the limestone, the ones that circle the town of Saumur, you're in the right place.

The Grapes

André Jullien is sometimes called the founder of modern wine writing. In his 1816 *Topographie de tous les vignobles connus* (*Topography of All Known Vineyards*) he wrote that "red wines constitute a very small portion of what the Anjou vineyards produce and are with some exceptions coarse and of low quality." There was one major exception, in Jullien's opinion: Champigny-le-Sec (the original name for the commune of Souzay-Champigny, about 15 minutes from the Clos Rougeard).

Jullien wrote that the area produced "full-bodied wines with a dark color, good taste and generous texture." He added that after four to five years of aging, they finally become expressive. In 1845, the ampelographer Alexandre-Pierre Odart seconded that emotion. "The Breton vine" (Breton is the old name for Cabernet Franc) "is a veritable Proteus, expressing the locality where it is planted. For example, in the small district of Champigny-le-Sec, where the vineyards are on limestone, the wine is outstanding (and higher priced than Bordeaux). Feel free to look around though, there's some marvelous wines to be had outside of Saumur-Champigny—such as around Puy-Notre-Dame, a new appellation with a long history, located towards the west of the region where there is more silex in the soil and a little more Cabernet Sauvignon.

WHO TO DRINK

- François Saint-Lô; Vin de France (organic)
- Domaine Cousin-Leduc/Olivier Cousin; Vin de France (biodynamic)
- Le Batossay/Baptiste Cousin; Vin de France (biodynamic)
- Les Jardins Esméraldins/Xavier Caillard; Vin de France (organic)
- La Tour Grise/Philippe Gourdon; Saumur, Puy-Notre-Dame, and Vin de France (biodynamic)
- Château de Fosse-Sèche; Saumur (biodynamic)
- Domaine du Collier; Saumur (organic)
- Domaine Andrée/Stéphane Erissé; Vin de France (organic)
- Domaine Mélaric; Saumur, Puy-Notre-Dame (organic)
- La Porte Saint Jean/Sylvain Dittière; Saumur-Champigny (organic)
- Clos Rougeard; Saumur-Champigny (organic)

Piemonte

When it comes to this region in Italy's northwest territory, I'm like a local dog with a Piemontese white truffle: all consumed, obsessed, and hormonally activated. I'm not alone in this, of course. As far back as 77 AD, Pliny the Elder noted in his *Natural History* that the area around the Tanaro River in the Langhe region was a place for good wines.

But while their charms were noted centuries ago, the raging success has only started to creep up since the 1950s, and now Piemonte excites a passion amongst its devotees for wines that speak to structure and expression.

The region has the Ligurian Sea about an hour to the west, and is flanked by France and Switzerland. But it also has the Alps looming over it, where the name and the micro-climates come from: *pie* = feet, *monte* = mountain.

And of course, it's beautiful. In the spring, the trees burst into bloom like freshly popped corn. Fragrant violets fill the vineyards. In the fall, there's the blinding fog that shrouds the region ominously. The landscape is crazily chopped up, and the vines are on the slopes. Red-roofed hilltop villages seem like vine-covered bubbles. Piemonte has a peaceful, regal beauty; an innate elegance, a mixture of northern cultures. It remains feistily Italian. And the wine? Oh yes, it speaks more of its struggle than easy sun. When it comes to wine and longevity, that is a good thing.

There are four major regions here. If you speed, Monferrato is an hour from the Milan airport. Here you avoid the monotony of vineyard monoculture with its mixed crop and all manner of fruit trees. In the fall, (unfortunately) the mosquitos move in, thanks to the rice paddies not too far away. But the wines, even if little-known, don't bite. They are earthy, savory, and fresh, especially the Freisa, Nebbiolo, and the DOCG Barbera. Flanking Turin is the clay- and limestone-heavy region of Asti. This gets the DOCG for Barbera, as well as its fizzy and slightly sweet Moscato (no comment). Roero, with its soils laden with gypsum (an ingredient in plaster of Paris), has yet to find its way, or even its champion, despite its location between Asti and Alba and it's ability to grow some credible Nebbioli. And, finally we arrive to the region's star, Langhe.

The Dirt

The soils here have their origin in the sea and the mountains. When the Padano Sea retreated about 16 million years ago, it left a collection of marine sediments and God-knows-what-else that accumulated over millions of years in the basin. The area's structuring and stratification began 1 million years later during the Miocene Epoch, when tensions from the Apennines and the Alps caused a mountainous collapse. Underneath it all, those bodies of marine animals decomposed and mixed with clay, becoming marls and gypsum.

Another factor for the region is more recent. About 65,000 years ago, the river Tanaro changed directions from northerly to easterly. This accelerated erosion and a division arose between the more marl-rich soils of the Langhe and the younger, sandier soils of Roero.

Within the Barolo zone, there are two major soil types separated by the Alba-Barolo road: the younger Tortonian calcareous marl on the west and the older Helvetian sandstone on the east. The marl is said to produce more feminine wines, while the sandstone is said to produce more longer-lived and stronger ones. But while these stereotypes could be true, since there are so many other variables such as vinification and farming, I trust you'll take those generalities with grains of salt.

The winters can be harsh, cold, and wet. Summers are hot. Falls are lingering and cool and this allows the grapes, especially the later-harvested Nebbiolo, to hang and ripen after the others have been picked.

The fog is also a factor, it starts as the cooler weather rolls in, further slowing down the ripening and perhaps also adding to the mystery. In the end, this soil births what might be the world's best white truffles and a red wine, where Nebbiolo surely is king, but do not deny the supporting cast of characters, they are marvelous.

The Grapes

If they had asked me, there would be no grapes like Pinot Noir, Cabernet, Merlot, or Chardonnay in Piemonte. While I have to admit that the Pinot can do quite well there, the truth of the region lies with their indigenous grapes that just don't really succeed anywhere else. About 35% of the acreage belongs to white wine. Moscato d'Asti, the sparkling sweet wine from Moscato, is only good from a few producers, such as Bera. There is some light and acidic Erbaluce, the favorite of some drinkers—for me, it is a little forgettable but pleasant enough. There's also Arneis, a low-acid variety that has never really moved me.

While most of the whites are minor league, there is one huge exception: Cortese. Grown in the southeastern portion of the DOC of Gavi, it is synonymous with its place. In the hands of some, like the bad boy rabble-rouser (and biodynamic since 1985) Stefano Bellotti with his Cascina degli Ulivi on those red, clay limestone soils, the Cortese grape shows a magnificent expression (and don't miss his Dolcetto or Nebbiolos either). Carussin makes a more polite version of Cortese blended with some Carica l'Asino, an old variety whose name means "load up the donkey."

But the reds. This is what you are here to drink.

DOLCETTO: Early-ripening and low in acid, this is one of the first of the big Piemonte three (Barbera, Dolcetto, and Nebbiolo) that makes it to the table. It's name means "little sweet," though it is neither, being in reality nicely tannic and sturdy. But no one lately can figure out what the wine is. A lot has been made in stainless steel, with no wood aging, and pushed out for an early drinker. It can be a totally gorgeous wine. There are places that are famed for it and receive the DOCG: Diano d'Alba, Dogliani, and Ovado, where it usually gets planted where others don't ripen. The best producers are probably also the best producers of Barolo and Barbaresco. If you find any from Rinaldi, Cappellano, Mascarello, or Roagna, for example, snap them up. Look also for Nicoletta Bocca's age-worthy variations from San Fereolo. While she is known for her Barberas, her Dolcettos are even more noteworthy, not released before eight years of aging so as to show the rustic greatness of the grape.

BARBERA: Barbera shows up in Lombardy and Emilia-Romagna. California went through a flirtation with it but the grape is mostly important in Piemonte where it is the most planted—even if it has been reduced by half over the past twenty years.

The reason for its popularity? It ripens two weeks later than the others, but still earlier than Nebbiolo. Traditionally, it was second in the hierarchy of drinking. Dolcetto for every day, Barbera for Sunday dinner, then Nebbiolo for something fancier, and finally Barolo and Barbaresco for grand occasions.

And as far as at the table, it is famed as the classic pizza wine because its ripeness coupled with acidity makes it unbeatable.

Barbera is said to have originated in the hills of Monferrato. Fabrizio Iuli, a champion of the grape in his region, says it excels on the loose soil, a mixture of clay, silt, and a significant amount of limestone. But, even though both Asti and Monferrato's Barbera can have DOCG status, the one from Asti remains more well-known.

As with Dolcetto and Nebbiolo (and often Freisa), most of the great Barolo and Barbaresco producers make small amounts of Barbera that are worth getting a hold of.

FREISA: Talk about a grape that gets no respect. It's shameful, given that this is one of the area's oldest, longest-lived grapes, and a cousin of Nebbiolo. It often falls into the "love it or loathe it" category in the grape tomes. The nice people say it is wild strawberry-like, but that is stretching the grape's charms into a profile that may or may not be true. The ones you're looking for are not the fizzy, frothy varieties but the rare vintages by winemakers who treat it the same way as they would Nebbiolo. It needs age for its natural tannins to mellow, and then it does get fruity on the nose with a long depth of pleasure. Look to some of the best Barolo producers who also make wonderful Freisa—Giuseppe Rindaldi Burlotto and Principiano Ferdinando are of note.

GRIGNOLINO: Here's another grape that gets no respect. You won't find much of it, and few people give it the love it needs. And Grignolino can be confusing; it defies acquiring color, and it can have aggressive tannins. This is why so much of it ends up, like Freisa, in sparkling throwaways or rosés, instead of giving it the respect it deserves. But there are some around if you dig deep, even if they are in minute amounts. Check out the one from Scarpa in Monferrato or from Asti, Trinchero, and Cascina 'Tavijn. Give them some time to age up, you'll have a surprise in store.

PELAVERGA: A rare beauty that we need to see more of. It's tricky to grow and needs to be picked immediately before it loses its lively acidity. Here is a Loire attitude with a Piemontese character. It has been maligned, dismissed as a silly little grape, but thankfully some people have raised it from the dead. As Levi Dalton said in the food quarterly *The Art of Eating*, "People seek Pelaverga for the very traits that nearly led to its demise," meaning no deep color, no deep structure, no heavy tannins, and a food-friendly pour. Do seek out those from Burlotto, Castello di Verduno, and Olek Bondonio.

RUCHÉ: Pronounced "roo-kay," this one is a charmer. And there's very little of it around, even though there's a DOCG for it in Castagnole Monferrato. There, in the hands of Cascina 'Tavijn, it is a wine of aromatic pleasure and density.

NEBBIOLO: Sheldon Wasserman mused in his 1990 book, *Italy's Noble Red Wines*, on the true identity of the grape Pliny had rhapsodized about, "a late-ripening and cold-resistant black grape." Pliny called it Allobrogica, but according to Wasserman, it sure sounded a lot like Nebbiolo.

This grape is luckily resistant to frost and stands up to the local fog, which is lucky. While some believe that's where the grape gets its name, the erudite writer Jancis Robinson opines that it's more likely because of the fog-like bloom that adheres to the variety.

Often, it's compared to Pinot Noir, not so much in taste as in how fussy it is to soil. It likes that marly clay and hillsides. Grown in all areas of northern Italy, but the name changes: it's called Chiavennasca in the Lombardia region of Valtellina. In the region of Alto Piemonte, it is called Spanna. In the Valle d'Aosta, it's Picotoner. No matter the name, Nebbiolo can provide wines of extreme beauty that can live certainly longer than thirty years, especially when grown in the right zones and in the right conditions and entitled to become Barolo and Barbaresco. When it's just right, it blends complex aromas and tastes of rose petal, tar, and fennel.

WHO TO DRINK

OUTSIDE OF THE LANGHE
- Iluli; Monferatto (organic)
- Migliavacca; Monferatto (organic)
- Antica Casa Vinicola Scarpa; Monferrato (sustainable)
- Vittorio Bera & Figli; Asti (organic)
- Trinchero; Asti (organic)
- Carussin; Asti (organic)
- Cascina 'Tavijn; Asti (organic)
- Cascina degli Ulivi; Gavi (biodynamic)

Barbaresco and Barolo

Barbaresco is produced just east of Alba, from the very same grape as Barolo and Nebbiolo; and in this compact area that produces only about a third of the quantity of Barolo, the vines are planted more in amphitheaters than on hills. Maybe it's my own perception but I always have the idea that I am being hugged by the vines there, as opposed to being on top of them.

The main townships are Barbaresco, Nieve, and Treiso, and as the vineyards are closer to the Tanaro River and thus richer, that might offer one reason why they ripen earlier than their slightly more elite neighbor. The soils are Tortonion, as with the west side of Barolo. It is said that the resulting wines are little less tannic, softer, perhaps more fruity. While they don't have the reputation of being as long-lived, that doesn't mean that they don't keep, only that they come around to drinking a bit sooner—and oh, they cost a little less. A drop less. This is not a bad thing.

Even though it is easy to talk of Barbaresco and Barolo by comparisons, it is important to drink these wines in their own right as they have their own identity, even if they echo similar hints of roses, tar, leather, and violet. The wines must be aged for a minimum of 26 months, with at least nine months in wood. The Riserva wines get fifty months before being released, with the same minimum nine months in oak.

Barolo was my gateway drug, and I certainly wasn't the first to discover it. Pliny can probably claim that honor. The 1968 Barolo I sipped in the year 1980, the year Barolo was given its DOCG status—one of the country's first— was life-changing, showing me the specific spiritual pull of fermented grape juice. But like much of Italy's wines, Barolo took a while to find itself. The modern era for Barolo started in the 1950s, when the region started to lock down a way to make a dry wine with consistency.

But in the late 1970s, something else happened: new barrels. And that was the beginning of a revolution that nearly wiped out the wines of both Barolo and Barbaresco. In an effort to make this wine drinkable earlier, in came the rotor-fermenters and other technology. People stopped making wine naturally and started using toasted Bordeaux barrels and even adding Cabernet Sauvignon to the wine to increase the purple color. The land split into the traditionalists and the modernists, with Bartolo Mascarello the most verbal of the traditionalists. The most public issue was trading in the large traditional oak and chestnut barrels called *botti* for the brand new barrels as used in Bordeaux, called *barrique.* These often left a hard texture and tastes like blueberry and vanilla. But there were other issues as well. The modernists tried to soften the wines before their time using many different kind of additives and new machines. The traditionalists? They clung to the old barrels that did not change the wine's flavors, worked with natural yeasts and more gentle methods in general. It's important to remember that this exalted area for the vine also birthed a fierce cluster of partisans who fought in their own way against fascism and Nazis and also made wine. Mascarello was one of them. At least in my mind, all this history, climate, landscape, and heroism helps to infuse the best of the wines with a complex and profound taste.

Mascarello died in 2005, but his capable daughter Maria Teresa is carrying on his tradition. Now the region is coming back to its senses, and more people are working in a way that allows the wine to reveal itself more naturally.

THE ELEVEN COMMUNES OF BAROLO

TO THE EAST OF THE ALBA/BAROLO ROAD WITH MORE SANDSTONE

- La Morra
- Barolo
- Castiglione Falletto
- Serralunga d'Alba
- Monforte d'Alba

TO THE WEST OF THE ALBA/BAROLO ROAD WITH MORE LIMESTONE

- Verduno
- Roddi
- Grinzane Cavour
- Diano d'Alba
- Novello
- Cherasco

What's in a Barolo DOCG

There are laws concerning how long a wine needs to be aged and in what kind of container. For a Barolo, here's the deal:

1. The wine must be 100 percent Nebbiolo.
2. Minimum alcohol is 13 percent.
3. Barolo requires 38 months of aging from November 1 of the harvest year, including 18 months of aging in wood.
4. Barolo Riserva requires 62 months of aging from November 1 of the harvest year, and at least 18 months in wood.
5. The vines must be planted at a minimum elevation of 170 meters and a maximum of 540 meters.
6. Complete northern exposures of vineyards are prohibited. (Note: They might want to rethink this, as in our currently changing climate, alcohols are getting very high with southern and western exposures.)
7. The yield is controlled at 56 hectoliters per hectare, and the vines must be at least seven years old. For a wine with the newly allowed designation of a single vineyard, "Vigna," the yields are even lower.

Winemaker Profile: Lorenzo Accomasso

As we tried to suss out which apartment was Lorenzo Accomasso's, I noticed some roosters doing a damned good imitation of a Chagall painting, perched on the roof of a coop's hut. We then walked into an open door, into a disheveled receiving room, and saw the baseball-capped, blue-eyed Barolo legend himself waiting for us.

Lorenzo Accomasso of La Morra is an outsider as well as a hold-out for tradition. The winemaker is now in his 70s, and only speaks in the Piemontese dialect. This is why Giorgio, a Piemontese man who lives in and imports wine into Australia (and wants Lorenzo for his portfolio) convinced Marta Rinaldi (the daughter of noted producer Giuseppe Rinaldi) to come along and interpret.

Accomasso talked slowly and poured even slower. He finally allowed us the dregs of two open bottles while he rattled on to Marta. I sipped. I scribbled: "These wines are my new heart-throbs."

Lorenzo is an elderly bad boy who makes thrilling wines, at least based on the two that I tasted that afternoon. I'd never had them before, as they are currently not available in the United States. I imagine they still linger on some wine lists, purchased in the days when Winebow was their stateside importer. But Lorenzo stopped that relationship fifteen years back. He found the process too much hassle—the back label, the front label, the rules and the red tape. His is old-fashioned, traditional Barolo, showing off all of that Barolo-ness that left me speechless before I had a wine vocabulary: the road tar, roses, licorice, and something like a fine sun-bleached Brooks bicycle seat. His fermentation occurs in cement vats for about 25 days, with maceration on the skins, then it goes into big old *botti*. Done.

"Those *barriquistas* used to try to convince me to use *barriques*," the sky blue-eyed winemaker said. Those *barriquistas* failed. It was obvious Accomasso is a stubborn guy who can't be convinced to do anything he doesn't want to do.

Something had happened in the middle of the translations, and Marta's voice changed. I saw she had started to pick her fingers and blush.

"What is he telling her?" I asked Giorgio.

He could make out a little of the conversation and whispered to me: "He said he had lots of girlfriends and women friends he'd have loved to take to bed but he didn't want to mess with the friendships."

Ah, I thought, the roosters weren't only on the roof. If Lorenzo was gunning for Marta, a clear 45 years his junior, then good luck to this fine winemaker with the missing teeth, sparkling eyes, and mischievous grin.

He finally poured us one more wine, the Rocche. It had more color, with a needly mouth, rustic edges, a touch of Good & Plenty candy and fresh salty air. "They're not polished," he said of his wines. Thank goodness for that.

But if you want to drink them, you'll have to go to Germany or Japan. Or better still, go knock on his door. His is brilliant stuff, but it's over when Accomasso is over. Seek him out. Bring cash. Or maybe just bring Marta instead.

WHO TO DRINK

BAROLO

- Cappellano (organic)
- Ferdinando Principiano (organic)
- Giuseppe Rinaldi (organic)
- Flavio Roddolo (organic)
- Roagna (organic)
- Brovia (sustainable)
- Giovanni Canonica (organic)
- Lorenzo Accomasso (sustainable)
- Bartolo Mascarello (organic)
- Scarpa (sustainable)

BARBARESCO

- Roagna (biodynamic)
- Cascina delle Rose (organic)
- Ca' Nova (organic)
- Roccalini (organic)
- Fabio Gea (organic)
- Produtorri del Barbaresco (conventional)

Rioja

I was standing in the midst of gnarled Tempranillo vines poking out of what seemed to be deep soil and a cobblestone road of river stones. White and yellow rocks the size of the cow knee bones my mother used to put in her tomato soup were scattered everywhere. A few feet down the slope, toward the river, was an abrupt transition into sandy soils. This is Rioja, a distinguished piece of Spain that almost no one talks about anymore. Over the past twenty years, they lost most of their old customers as they pursued making more conventional-tasting wines—and losing their soul in the process. But no worries, they picked up plenty of others and is the most known region in the country.

About 100 miles southeast of Bilbao in north central Spain, Rioja is a relatively new wine region. There's evidence that the Romans made wine there, and there was also a local industry in the 15th century. But it was in the 1860s when Rioja came to prominence, thanks to phylloxera. When the louse decimated Bordeaux, the winemakers at the top of the wine game needed to find a place to plant vines and to bring in wines. Rioja had access to the ocean—at least the town of Haro, which became a locus of wine activity, was. The region was an hour's train ride from the Atlantic, and from there it was an easy sail to Bordeaux. The French came en masse, brought their small barrels, and started businesses and relations. But the Spanish found American oak was cheaper, and that distinct taste helped to define the Riojan style. In the 1900s, when Bordeaux was back on its feet, it was Rioja's turn to get hit by the pest. There went the vines. Ouch. The vines in the sandy soils were safe, since phylloxera can't abide sand. But under those limestone, quartz, rocks was a mix of limestone and clay, and the pest feasted. Bye-bye, Rioja. Rioja discovered, as did the rest of the world, that they needed to graft the vine onto the roots of American vines, which were immune, instead of directly planting into the soil as in the past. There were ups and downs, fungus and Civil War, then World War II, and Franco. Finally, modern Spanish wine came into its own around the 1960s, only to find another problem thirty years later: modernization.

The Dirt

Rioja is a mix of climates and microclimates, so it's really hard to generalize. Is it Atlantic cool and wet? Is it Mediterranean hot and dry or continental, with swings between hot and cold? A little of all three profiles apply to this region, which sits in a bumpy bowl between two mountain ranges, the Cantabrian Mountains to the north and the Sierra de la Demanda to the south. Within, there are seven rivers and seven valleys carving up its terrain. There are numerous microclimates, and often harvest doesn't come around until October.

There are three pieces to the Rioja puzzle. Rioja Alta is where most of the vines around Haro, the center for the Rioja explosion in the 1800s, exist. These are mostly limestone mixed with clay and alluvial sand. The Alavesa is just north, higher elevation with the highest concentration of calcareous clay soils. Then there is the southern part, Rioja Baja, east of the city of Logroño. Here it's iron-laced clay and alluvial, warmer and flatter and often seen as a lesser place for wine with more Grenache than Tempranillo. Not saying that some wines can't be made there, but in Rioja, where there is limestone, it just seems to be finer.

López de Heredia is a much-loved Haro winery with roots stretching back to the 1800s. Run by María José López de Heredia, her sister Mercedes, and their brother Julio César, they are vocal about not having changed any element of their winemaking since their great-grandfather. Julio took me into the vines, anchored in varied soil, with dips and turns in the topography, ranging from big white boulders to silky sand. "Sand gives structure, limestone slow maturation," he said. Taking me high up to their Alavesa site, where they get their grapes for their Cubillo, the vine's struggle on the pure chalk was obvious.

"We're between the Mediterranean and the Atlantic," said Jorge Muga, a winemaker from another venerable house. "So we could be classified as either. The thing about Rioja," Muga said, "is that terroir is more dominant than the grape."

That might be, but it's not more dominant than technique or process. The process, characterized by long aging in American oak for up to three years (longer for the wines of López de Heredia) marks the wine. Yet one could recognize it as Rioja because of the spiced wood and old bureau kind of odors. But in a truly traditional wine, the flavors of chicken soup and dill, with touches of iron, blood, and depth, were all in balance. Today's techniques, using super-ripe grapes (especially Grenache from Baja) and technology engaged to make sure the wine tastes the same— yeasts, enzymes, micro-oxygenation, concentrators—have made the wines chunky and inelegant. "My grandmother," Muga said, "was a great winemaker. She could blind taste her way through all of the wines from the villages. Today? I can't tell the differences in continent!"

The Grapes

If there was one grape that was known as the grape of Spain, here it is: Tempranillo. This is an early-ripener, and it's grown all around Spain with different names such as Tinto Fino, Tinto del País, Tinta de Toro, Ull de Llebre, and Cencibel and in Portugal, Tinta Roriz. It's a grape that is sensitive to drought and wind, which makes it an odd one as so much of Spain is parched in the summer. And yet it thrives. Outside of Iberia it rarely shows up, though there's some grown on granitic soil in the Sierra Nevada Foothills and in Australia.

Garnacha or Grenache, however you want to call it, is everywhere in warm climates, from France to Australia. It zooms to high alcohol all too quickly, and traditional vintages, such as Châteauneuf-du-Pape, relied on other grapes (including some whites) to balance it out. Here, too, blending has been traditional, using grapes like Mazuelo (also known as Cariñena or Carignan) and the white grapes of Malvasia and white Garnacha. The deeply colored and perfumed Graciano, like Carignan, is another acid protector, though perhaps a little dull all on its own. Maturana Tinta, (Bastardo in Portugal and Trousseau in the Jura) is a minor player.

White wines used to be made here, and they were fascinating. These were long-aged whites from Viura (aka Macabeo) and Malvasia. You can still find the real McCoy in those from López de Heredia. God bless them, they're the only ones serving up the tastes of the past. Their whites age longer than their reds, and so do their rosés. Their gran reserva, for example, is aged ten years in American oak and nine years in the bottle. For those expecting fresh fruit flavors, forget it. Instead, you'll find a nutty, caramelized, spicy number.

Historically, the Riojan bodegas released their wines only when they were ready to drink. This is less so now, and the long aging rules have been relaxed, though some traditional bodegas like López de Heredia still follow the traditional classifications. The code for the red wines are as follows:

1. Joven: A new wine. Emphasis on freshness.
2. Crianza: Wines that are at least in their third year, having spent a minimum of one year in casks. For white wines, the minimum cask aging period is six months.
3. Reserva: Selected wines of the best vintages with an excellent potential that have been aged for a minimum of three years, with at least one year in casks.

4. Gran Reserva: Selected wines from exceptional vintages which have spent at least two years in oak casks and three years in the bottle. For white wines, the minimum aging period is four years, with at least one year in casks.

- López de Heredia (sustainable)
- Contino (organic)
- La Rioja Alta (conventional)
- Honorio Rubio (sustainable)
- Viña Ilusión (organic)
- Akutain (organic)
- Abel Mendoza (organic)
- Olivier Riviere (organic)

In general, anything that you see prior to the 1990 vintage is worth giving a try.

So why spend this much time on a region with so many modern wines? Because it all matters: The soils. The climate. The history. Rioja will rise again.

SILEX (FLINT)

There's an awful lot of silex, commonly known as flint or chert, in the eastern central part of the Loire. Certainly in Montlouis-sur-Loire and Vouvray, but especially where Sauvignon Blanc is grown in Pouilly-Fumé and Sancerre. In Sancerre, it makes up 15 percent of the landscape, mostly located closer to the Loire River on the east side of that hilly and complex appellation. Some people believe that this addition to mostly limestone soils gives the wines their extra smokiness. Try them from Alexandre Bain Dagueneau and Jonathan Pabiot in Pouilly Fumé, Sebastian Riffault, Domaine Vacheron, Domaine Vatan, and Vincent Gaudry, and try to imagine the smell of a knife being drawn from a warrior's side. "It is from the Sauvignon Blanc on silex I get white truffles and peaches and a distinct minerality," Gaudry says. From his flintier soils, he claims, he gets a blend of sweet earth and fruit aromas with a strong lingering vibrancy, a kind of fruit in the wine that needs to be teased out. But is it true? Pascaline had this to say: "The flint-stone [silex] which can make the soil quite bright or give it a soft orange hue, often gets the credit for giving wines flint-like aromas. I can agree with that. Take Chenin on silex, like in Vouvray with Philippe Foreau or François Pinon (who has his cuvées named after his soils, including a Silex Noir), whose wines have a distinct smoked salt, gunpowder element. The flavors might be due to the heat absorption by the flint-stones in the sun."

There's also more silex down southwest, north of Toulouse in the town of Fronton, which is known for currently inexpensive wines made from Négrette, Domaine Le Roc, and Chateau Plaisance.

SHALE (MUDSTONE)

The somewhat secret terroir of shale might be threatened by the increasing use of fracking, but some damned interesting soils have this strange rock that you can almost watch in transition. The Finger Lakes in upstate New York might be fighting off the shale rigs to keep their vines safe, and so far (fingers crossed), they are beginning to deliver on the promise of this remarkable cool climate area. Eleven narrow lakes stretch out like the fingers on a hand. On their steep banks once covered with American grapes like Concord, Delaware, or Catawba, now grow vinifera. Hermann J. Wiemer has been working well up in those parts;

Element Winery, Bellweather, Nathan Kendall, and Shaw Vineyard are also worth looking into. Seek out Bloomer Creek for the most unadulterated expression of Riesling, Cabernet Franc, and soon Chenin.

One of the most amazing shale soils I've seen was high in the Santa Cruz mountains, on Mount Eden at the Martin Ray vineyard. This was the site of one of the first plantings of Pinot Noir in the United States. Now the duo of Arnot-Roberts, a Sonoma-based winery, is making some remarkable, savory Pinot Noirs from this very historical site.

Of special note is Italy's Tuscan region of Montalcino, the land where the special clone of Sangiovese (called Sangiovese Grosso) becomes the famed Brunello wine.

I was with Francesca Padovani, who farms and makes a wine called Fonterenza with her twin sister, Margarita. We were walking in one of their vineyards on a powerfully sunny day when she pulled me over to a hillside and started to flake away at the rock and a storm of papery shards started to fall, not unlike schists, which would have been the next step into metamorphosis. "*Galestro*," she said of the soil that had been baked in the Tuscan sun until it turned into brittle, friable mineral sheets. Makers of Brunello you'll want to look for are the Fonterenza, Cerbaiona, the breathtakingly priced Soldera, and Stella di Campalto.

There is a related although confusing relative up north in the odd clay and limestone soils of Friuli in the subregion called the Friuli Colli Orientali region, so close to Slovenia. The place, a famous one for a cluster of intriguing winemakers, is called Oslavia.

One of them is Radikon. Saša Radikon, the son of the late, widely loved vintner, Stanko, is a good-natured man with a brittle brush of a haircut. With dinner cooking upstairs, he took me down to the cellar. There in back of the huge barrels where wines were aging up was a wall of . . . mud and clay. Or what looked like it. It was mudstone that was way harder to the touch than it looked. Soils of this kind has the ability to hold and release great amounts of water. Many of the wines of Friuli are from Merlot and another red grape called Refosco, which is thought to make a sturdy red wine, especially when paired with soils that appear to be from many eons later in time, breakable slats of sandstone. Where shale will break into sheets, these mudstones will break horizontally. Their whites are Sauvignon, Tocai Friulano, Malavasia, Pinot Grigio, and Ribolla Gialla. Over the past twenty years, white wines made from skin contact—white wines made like red wines, which emerge with an orange or amber color—have become increasingly familiar. You'll want to look for the wines of Radikon, Josko Gravner, Damijan Podversic, and Dario Prinčič.

HEAVY CLAY

Abruzzo is in the midlands east of Italy; it starts at the Adriatic Sea and then reaches west to the Apennines. The soils are derived from calcareous clay—with the emphasis on clay. I was in the fine vineyards of Emidio Pepe, a prime example of the specific soils in the Torano Nuovo. It was 2014, long regarded as a flood year of unparalled proportions. While the season just past harvest dried out the soils like quicksand and then became as hard as cement. Working those soils? Intense. But the structure of the wines Emidio Pepe extracts? Noble. While much of Abruzzo is known for wines that are to be drunk and perhaps not that important, Pepe's wines defy the reputation and show what the soils paired with the right grapes can become. These are long-lived wines, both whites and reds. The white grapes the area is known for are Trebbiano and Pecorino. The former silky, the latter gritty. And of course the Montepulciano d'Abruzzo is the red grape.

GRAVELS

Bordeaux

The Romans planted the first vines in Bordeaux about 2,000 years ago and the area in the southwest of France has defined fine wine ever since. But starting from the 1600s when the Dutch shipping merchants expanded the vineyard area by draining the swamp to reveal more of its esteemed terroir, and the British thirst for their claret was unquenchable, their star has mostly risen. Today, the top wines of the region have been increasingly associated with commodities. Like stock or any investment, they are bought for resale value. That is a tragedy and has nearly castrated the region's soul.

The region is separated into left and right banks—depending on which side of the Gironde Estuary they sit. The scene was set back in 1855 when properties on the left bank in the greater area now called the Médoc, the Graves and the Sauternais (from where the sweet Sauternes come from), were given "growth" status, as in 1st to 5th. These were given to landowners, châteaus with their vines around the property. Not to the villages or vineyards themselves as in other regions. In the past fifty years these special properties have become increasingly commercial and only now on the verge of changing their farming practice and questioning their modernization, but mostly just not worthy. However, they are historical. The region is historical. The land is the reason Cabernet Sauvignon and Blanc and Merlot are so ubiquitous and mimicked the world over. All passionate wine drinkers need to know the basics here.

The netherworld between the left and right bank is the Entre-Deux-Mers (known mostly for whites of Sauvignon Blanc). On the right bank, the eastern side of the Dordogne, are the villages of Pomerol and Saint-Émilion. Lesser-known regions, where you can stumble on some respectful wines, include Fronsac, Côtes de Castillon, Côtes de Blaye, and Côtes de Bourg. One can find the bulk of the committed folk doing more of the work in the soil and less of the work in the cellars.

On the left bank, you've heard the names: Lafite-Rothschild, Latour, and Mouton-Rothschild from the village of Pauillac, Margaux from Margaux, and Haut-Brion from Pessac. Those five are the first growth (out of five) and are treated as are any blue chip stock. With stratospheric prices, most mortals will never be able to taste them, and in my humble opinion pretty much only the wines pre-1986 are worth lusting for. Since 1982 they've been leaving behind a savory, complex leanness with a compelling somewhereness and creeping toward a California wannabe style of fruit and oak. They've ditched the elegance that made these wines formidable, long-lived, and capable of fascinating evolution.

That doesn't mean that today's wines should to be ignored. The entire region with all of its smaller appellations could use a little love, and there are lovely people working the various soils, and after all, it's the most famous example of gravel. So, I give you Bordeaux.

The Dirt

A few miles away from the Atlantic Ocean, in a C-curve in France, is the humid and maritime region. More water influence comes from the Gironde estuary that splits off into tributaries of the Garonne and the Dordogne. I remember on my first visit to the region, a cab driver picking me up in the city of Bordeaux said with derision for the locals, "swamp people." I was taken aback, but she was clear that she felt her home city of Saint-Émillion was superior. She was, of course, referring to the large part of the Médoc exposed by the Dutch during the big drain.

The land is varied. It can be flat and boring. It can be rural and peaceful. There can be stretches of green hills, rocky, gravelly soils. The best terroirs are on croupes (little hills), or on slopes and plateau, especially around the picturesque medieval town of Saint-Émillion, which is directly on Pacific limestone full of marine fossils.

Being in the middle of all of those rivers and the retreating Atlantic, the city of Bordeaux and environs is perched above a giant mass of gravel, with variations of clay, sand, and, underneath, limestone. But it is the gravel that gets the most play. Gravel provides drainage in this humid and wet climate. The rocks also absorb the heat and allow for better ripening, but the ripening ability and how much clay is in the mix has a lot to do with what grows best. The left bank has more oceanic influences, moderating the warmth in the summer and the cold in the winter. There is more gravel and clay so more Cabernet Sauvignon and Merlot. The right bank is more continental with more limestone, better for Cabernet Franc and Merlot. Merlot can grow just about anywhere just as long as there's clay; the soils are heavier with clay on the right bank, hence more Merlot-heavy wines.

Those clay and limestone variations continue through the villages that begin to take on the famed names. The flat, two-and-a-half-mile square of Pomerol (famous for Petrus and Lafleur) has clay over limestone and sandy loam with pockets of iron deposits. It is this kind of deposit, referred to as *crasse de fer*—rotted iron—that defines the best wines of the area. The wines can be firm with delicacy and, when they come from the *crasse*, profound. From the website of Château Lafleur comes this explanation, they give "the wines a very characteristic flavour of something fat and metallic, which many associate with truffles."

A quick ride takes one over to the higher elevation of the picture-perfect town of Saint-Émilion (heard of Château Cheval Blanc, Ausone or Figeac?). There, happy on the limestone—just as it is in the Loire—Cabernet Franc takes dominance.

The Grapes

Cabernet Sauvignon and Merlot, the two most famous red grapes in the world, often imitated, come from these humid shores. While other expressions make people happy (I personally appreciate Merlot from the limestone soils of the Alto Adige in Italy) this is their home ground.

Both have one parent in common, Cabernet Franc. The other for Cabernet Sauvignon is the white Sauvignon Blanc. For Merlot, the other parent is still a mystery. Cabernet Sauvignon is late-ripening so it needs that longer time on the vine and does better on the poor gravel soils of the left bank. Merlot is mid-ripening, so it does well on the warmer right bank, where it is dominant. The other approved red grapes are Petit Verdot, Malbec, and Carménère. The main white grapes allowed are Sémillon, Sauvignon Blanc and Muscadelle, all of which are used for the sweet wines as well as the dry whites. Also allowed but more rarely seen are Sauvignon Gris, Ugni Blanc, Colombard, and Merlot Blanc.

WHO TO DRINK

RIGHT BANK

- Château La Grave/Paul Barre; Fronsac (biodynamic)
- Moulin Pey-Labrie; Fronsac (organic)
- Château Gombaude; Guillot-Pomerol (biodynamic)
- Château Belle-Brise; Pomerol (organic)
- Maison-Blanche; Montagne-Saint-Émilion (biodynamic)
- Château Meylet; Saint-Émilion (biodynamic)
- Château Fonroque; Saint-Émilion (biodynamic)
- Clos Puy Arnaud; Côte de Bordeaux (biodynamic)
- Château Le Puy; Côte de Bordeaux (biodynamic)
- Château Peybonhomme Les Tours; Côte de Bordeaux (biodynamic)
- Château La Grolet; Côtes de Bourg (biodynamic)
- Les Trois Petiotes; Côte de Bourg (organic)

LEFT BANK AND GRAVES

- Domaine du Jaugaret; Saint-Julien (organic)
- Clos du Jaugueyron; Margaux (organic, biodynamic)
- Château Pontet-Canet; Pauillac (organic, biodynamic)
- Château Massereau; Barsac and Graves (organic)

- Les Closeries des Moussis; Haut Médoc (organic)

OTHER SMALLER BORDEAUX APPELLATIONS
- Château du Champ des Treilles; Sainte-Foy-Bordeaux (organic)
- Château Tire Pé; Entre-Deux-Mers (organic)
- Jacques Broustet/Château Lamery Bordeaux (biodynamic)

DO NOT FORGET THE NEARBY REGIONS (LIMESTONE WITH AND WITHOUT GRAVEL)
- Château Jonc-Blanc; Bergerac (biodynamic)
- Domaine Mouthes Le Bihan; Côtes de Duras (organic)
- Élian da Ros; Côtes du Marmandais (biodynamic)
- Domaine du Pech; Buzet (biodynamic)
- Clos Siguier; Cahors (organic)
- Domaine Cosse-Maisonneuve; Cahors (biodynamic)
- Clos d'un Jour; Cahors (organic)
- Fabien Jouves/Mas del Périé; Cahors (biodynamic)

DIATOMACEOUS ROCK

Another little-known rock that fascinates is diatomaceous rock, or kieselguhr. This highly sought-after rock provides one of the main ingredients in water filters, cat litter, and toothpaste. But it can be also great for growing grapes. The sommelier-turned-winemaker Raj Parr illustrated this for me when he took a piece of it from his Santa Rita Hills vineyard and poured water on it. It was like a magic trick: the rock totally absorbed the moisture. White as chalk, diatomite has almost nothing to do with calcium carbonate. Like the latter, it is a marine sedimentary rock, but it's 90 percent silica from the fossilized bits of diatoms, a type of algae. Thus, diatomaceous soils need a lot of composting to help the vines grow, retain some water, and create humus. There are very few places in the world with this soil, especially in its pure state. Parr's young vineyard in Santa Barbara is full of this magic rock, which might help along his efforts for dry farming in that hot area.

And then there's Jerez in Spain. Jerez has the most peculiar, eccentric soils, with dazzling shards of what is often called chalk, but this is a blend of limestone with a huge abundance of diatoms. The Spanish call their soil *albariza* and it has a remarkable ability to absorb moisture. Ramiro Ibáñez Espinar, a consultant in the area, said that all *albariza* isn't the same but the content of fossils in the diatoms are essential to the absorbtion. This is one of those rare parts of the world where those diatoms meet calcium carbonate.

Sherry is made in Jerez from the Palomino grape, raised without fear of oxygen in barrels so flor yeast develops, just as it does in the Jura. After fermentation, the wine is fortified with the addition of neutral spirit. For sherry, be prepared for savory over fruit and open your mouth and enjoy. The wines are marked by great saltiness, with warming nutty and dried fruit accents. Look for these wonderful examples: Gómez Nevado, Equipo Navazos, Fernando de Castilla, and Valdespino.

THE SEDIMENTARY TASTING BOX

1. **Alice and Oliver de Moor, Aligoté Plantation 1902; Chablis, France (limestone)**

   The smell of the ocean breeze. This wine stretches. It has long strides, but there's that bracing acidity that is felt at the side of the mouth. Yet it is still so ripe and lush with a slightly grainy texture.

2. **Alice and Oliver de Moor, Chablis Bel-Air et Clardys; Chablis, France (limestone)**

Fresh, with the smell of Meyer lemon and a touch of flower and, I hate to admit it, but there's also some smoky flintiness. There's texture here. It's not plump, but there's a little give. The two De Moors hail from just meters away from one another, but here there's more limestone in the mix for the Chablis. This wine, as this is Chardonnay and not Aligoté, is broader, with less structure and a grainy texture.

3. **Francis Boulard & Fille, Les Murgiers Blanc de Noirs; Champagne, France (chalky limestone and clay)**

A gorgeous blanc de noir from 70% Pinot Meunier and 30% Pinot Noir, the nose has a voracious creamy energy that is pure and direct, with a very ripe lime-like acidity.

4. **François Chidaine, Les Choisilles; Montlouis-sur-Loire, France (tuffeau, clay, and silex)**

Chenin on limestone has this singing, passionfruit, yuzu-like quality, hitting from front to back. A touch of rhubarb, too, in the cooler vintages. Some sugars are usually left to balance out this acidity. And the finish is all about smoked salt, with a grainy, tannic, crabapple skin quality.

5. **Domaine Chandon De Briailles, Savigny-lès-Beaune or Pernand-Vergelesses; Burgundy, France (limestone and clay)**

Chardonnays from this part of Burgundy, on the border of Côtes de Nuits and de Beaune, have aromatics driven by aging and the work on the lees. The wine is really about a sour cream, yogurt-like quality with that acid tension, very centered in the palate. The fat of some vintages may hide it, but in this wine it is here, and provides structure. When from old vines, the finish can remind you of reduced chicken broth.

6. **Domaine Jean-François Ganevat, Les Grandes Teppes Vieilles Vignes; Jura, France (red marl and gravel)**

Broad and boisterous up front, a rich Chardonnay that hides a fantastic acidity, the soil seems to give richness and tension at the same time. Definitely exotic, a touch of oxidation, a beast to tame and wait for it to lose its baby fat.

7. **Domaine Charvin, Châteauneuf-du-Pape; Rhône Valley, France (gravels)**

A blend of mostly Grenache with bits of Mourvèdre, Carignan, Syrah, and an ancient minor player, Vaccarèse. The vines are planted in clay and on a bed of galets roulés—those smooth stones that were washed down from the Alps. This comes from a cooler section of the warm Châteauneuf region, there's more freshness to the wine. Still, it is powerful. This is a whole-cluster fermentation in cement and the wine gives full on red fruit and sun while the mid palate is restrained and the finish gives great, tea-like, ripe licorice-like tannins.

8. **Campi di Fonterenza, Rosso Di Montalcino; Tuscany, Italy (paper shale)**

The Sangiovese Grosso is picked from Francesca's goblet vines on rotted rock—paper shale soils, which they call galestro—the grapes are destemmed, vinified in stainless and Slavonian oaks, and then aged in that combination for two years. The result it textural, a heavy silk with touches of forest fruit and frank deliciousness. The acidity is heightened, similar to the Cubillo.

9. **López de Heredia, Cubillo; Rioja, Spain (chalk and clay)**

The Tempranillo from chalk and high altitude shows such a different face than one than from land by the rivers. It has a dusty berry on the nose, with bramble and subtle fruits on the palate. The tannins are subtle,

more like corduroy than sandpaper. Behind the fruit, there's this high note
of acid that is very different from the López de Heredia wines from lower
altitude and with less chalk in the soil.

Aligoté, Chardonnay, and Chenin—taste and compare. Three grapes, similar families of bedrock limestone from different epochs, and all express their acids in different ways. Move on to the reds: Pinot Noir, Grenache, Sangiovese Grosso, and Tempranillo from benchmark producers and disparate climes. For fun, taste a Côte de Nuits of your choosing alongside the Savigny. For example, look for one of Amélie Berthaut's (Domaine Berthaut) Fixin—Les Cras or Les Clos—and compare the textures.

Acidity: This is a high-toned quality, very lifted, similar to orange or tangerine for ripe acids. Check if it is all in balance with the fruit. Or does it knock the wine off its feet?

Texture: In the mouth, is the wine razor-sharp, focused, and linear?

Tannins: Are they round? Soft? Edgy and rustic, or precise and just a touch chalky?

Sedimentary Cheat Sheet

Where	Soils	Climate	Known For
France: Burgundy	limestone, clay	continental; cold wet winter, warm summer	Pinot Noir, Chardonnay, Aligoté
France: Jura	limestone, clay	continental; cold winter, warm summer	Chardonnay, Savagnin, Poulsard, Trousseau, Pinot Noir
France: Touraine, Loire	limestone, clay, flint, alluvial	moderate, somewhere between Atlantic and continental, wet, mild	Chenin, Sauvignon Blanc, Romorantin, Cabernet Franc, Pinot Noir, Côt, Grolleau, Gamay, Pineau d'Aunis

France: Sancerre and Pouilly-Fumé	limestone, silex	moderate, wet, mild	Sauvignon Blanc
France: Bordeaux	limestone, clay, gravel	wet, oceanic influence	Cabernet, Merlot, Petite Verdot, Malbec, Sémillon, Muscadelle, Sauvignon Blanc
Italy: Piemonte	limestone, sandstone	cold winters, warm summers, rain and fog	Nebbiolo, Barbera, Dolcetto, Freisa, Ruché, Grignolino
Italy: (NW) Montalcino and Chianti	limestone, galestro	warm, sunny	Sangiovese Grosso
Spain: Rioja (Alavesa, Alta)	limestone, sand	mixed oceanic and mountain influence; warm, sunny, rain	Tempranillo, Garnacha, Gaciano, Mazuelo, Maturana Tinta, Viura, Malvasia
Spain: Jerez	chalk, diatomite	hot, Mediterranean	Palomino, Pedro Ximenez
Slovenia: Primorska	limestone	continental with cold, wet winters	Vitovska, Rebula Teran, Refošk, Merlot, Malvazia
Georgia: Imereti	limestone, clay	rainy, cool	Tsolikauri, Tsitska, Otskhanuri Sapere
Georgia: Khaheti	sandstone, limestone	hot, desert-like	Saperavi, Rkatsiteli, Kisi
USA: Santa Cruz, California	shale	hot and dry days, cool at night	Pinot Noir, Chardonnay, Cabernet
USA: Santa Rita Hills, California	diatomite	hot and dry days, cool at night	Pinot Noir, Chardonnay
USA: Finger Lakes, New York	shale	cold winter, warm summer, rain	Riesling, Chardonnay, Cabernet Franc, Pinot Noir

CHAPTER 3

METAMORPHIC

In Kafka's *The Metamorphosis*, poor Gregor Samsa went to bed as a man and woke up as a roach. It helps to remember that dramatic change when pondering the lineage of metamorphic rocks. After all, they too used to be something else. But their transformation took millions of years of heat and pressure, not a mere single night.

In taste terms, in metamorphic-derived soils you can get broad flavors, the rich and the powerful. Put the rock and vine in the sun and the heat and the resulting wines can be explosive. In the wet and the cool, they can prove a little shier, but still plump in the mouth. Those rocks create thicker skins, which sometimes can be a problem for red grapes. Heat or cool, wet or dry, what they have in common are these textures that spread across the mouth in a filling way.

Metamorphics are grouped into two categories: non-foliated and foliated. The Latin origin of the word foliate is *folium*, meaning leaf. In geological terms, it refers to the way the minerals are aligned in the rock. Each layer of rock might be as thin as a sheet of paper, akin to the mille-feuille (literally "thousand leaf") pastry of France or the phylo pastry of Greece. So a non-foliated rock is one piece, with no layering. Non-foliated metamorphic rocks have a pretty uniform appearance. Hornfels, marble, quartzite, and amphibolite are non-foliated. Hornfels, a bastard child, can come from just about anything, but its most often thought of as originating from siliceous shale mud. Amphibolite is mostly metamorphosed from the igneous and generally has a high percentage of iron and magnesium. Marble and lapis are easy to trace; they both descended from limestone.

The many layers of foliated rocks can be found in slate, phyllite, schist, and gneiss. Gneiss, which can morph from volcanic, granite, or schist, often has strikingly visible stripes coursing through the stone. Slate and schist are profoundly important rocks when it comes to grape soil. They come from a younger type of sedimentary rock: shale. Though these siblings might lie close to each other on the geological family tree, they are as different as Cain and Abel.

SLATE AND SCHIST

Dark and brittle, slate has an almost neutral pH. Fragile, formed under lesser pressure and heat than schist, it is less compressed. Slate dazzles with different textures and colors, including brown, red, black, and blue. In the Priorat region, in eastern Spain two hours or so from Barcelona, they call their particular brand of slate (which looks like large copper shards weathered in the hot sun) *llicorella*. In Germany's Mosel, especially, the pieces are longer and broader and come in a multitude of colors. There, they call them *schiefer*, but don't differentiate between slate and schist. In the Mosel, the soil is just one metamorphic blur.

Schist often has a higher pH than slate and a greater density. Like slate, it comes in all sorts of shades, including black, blue, and silver. Unlike slate, it can present itself in bold, hard forms such as over on the northern Atlantic region of Spain's Ribeira Sacra, where it's called *lousas*. The Roussillon, in the south of France, has two kinds of schist: the type that looks like broken stone mats, called *dalles*, and more slender fragments called *frites*.

But what does schist and slate mean for the vine and wine? The best schist and slate soils are layered at right angles to the Earth's surface rather than horizontally. This affects the way the water can seep in directly, which is essential as, depending on how much clay there is in the decomposed stone, the soil can have very poor retention. Also those kinds of soils erode more quickly, especially if there are winter freezes, as in the Mosel in Germany. This makes it easier for the roots to dig deep into the ground for a good drink of water.

Terroir expert Pedro Parra believes that no matter what the climatic conditions, the wines from grapes grown in schist are big wines. They can also show a streak of iron alongside powerful tannins. But how does schist and slate affect each of our favorite regions, such as the Loire, the south of France, and Iberia?

The Loire and Anjou Noir

The story of the town of Angers is a tale of two soils: the tuffeau limestone Anjou Blanc and the dark schist and slate of Anjou Noir. While they both produce exciting wines, they can be markedly different. The grape that experiences the greatest discrepancy on these two soils is Chenin. Some have described Chenin on schist and slate as fleshier and more savory than its limestone-grown counterparts. There are some who get nasty, though, saying that the Chenin on the dark rocks is austere, powerful, bitter, and "intellectual." One of these would be French wine critic Michel Bettane. He is on record likening Chenin on schist to "stale choucroute, old cheese rind, rancid butter, moldy dough."

While Bettane is vociferous in his dislike of Chenin on schist, the critic Andrew Jefford made a passionate case for it in his marvelous book *The New France*. He's not alone; Anjou-raised Pascaline and I love it. Far from Bettane's description, we find that the best Chenin Blancs from schist have a deep, violet and quince complexity with a round, plump, grainy, juicy fullness. Like them or love them—and it's best you do a tasting and find out where you fall—there are concrete reasons why they taste so very different.

Sponge-like tuffeau performs better in dry years. It has what it takes to hold on to whatever rain does fall. Meanwhile, in the cool, wet years, it is the schist that does best, with its great capacity to hold on to warmth, yet let go of the rain, providing better drainage.

Looking for more answers, I went to talk to the winemakers themselves. I often tasted with Kenji and Mai Hodgson. These expats from Vancouver settled in the thriving village of Faye-d'Anjou to make wine. They are young and newish, but their wine's vitality has always impressed me.

Faye-d'Anjou was once known exclusively for its sweet wines, and now has a clutch of super fine winemakers who are ultra-natural in their approach. "The Saumur whites don't usually go through the malo," Kenji explained, mentioning the malolactic fermentation that usually follows alcoholic fermentation and softens the acids, adding a fleshy roundness. "This is possibly because the colder cellar temperatures of the troglodyte caves inhibit it." Another reason that malo is naturally inhibited is that limestone soils are lower in pH than schist and higher in acid, and that can be inhospitable to malolactic bacteria.

Hodgson posited that some of the Saumurois might choose to block the malo (often with sulfur dioxide and cold) in order to give the wines the impression of more acid. This is something committed minimalist winemakers in the area would never forcefully do, and there are a lot of natural winemakers in the Anjou. "So," he said, "we in the Noir are left with a softer acidity [lactic] rather than a tangier one, or mineral or tension or whatever you might call it." Hence, the wines can be softer and less angular.

But there are factors at play that conspire to make a different kind of wine. There's humidity from the three main rivers, the Loire, the Layton, and the Aubance. The protection from the southwestern rains by the Massif des Mauges south of the Layon, which makes this part of Anjou one of the warmest, driest spots of all the Loire Valley, boosts the wine's alcohols. The humid wind blows up as if in a funnel from the Atlantic which helps to dry out the soils, especially if it's a year when there's not that much rain. So with all these conditions, Botrytis—that rot which concentrates the sugars in a grape—has been part of the landscape of Anjou Noir's wines, much more than in the Anjou Blanc, which is located more inland and has less humidity and fog influence. It is because of this remarkable affinity for the noble rot that his region is one of the world's holy grails for sweet wine. Likewise, the fame of the area's sweet wines has long overshadowed the region's dry examples. However, in the current situation, dry Chenin is in a major growth phase and have become one of the area's most exciting developments.

What was behind such a display of disgust for Chenin on schist from Bettane? Was it his preference for a more lean and mean wine that got him so disgruntled with the schistic dry Chenin? Or is he just a staunch traditionalist who wants the wines of that area to accept the Botrytis and for the Anjou Noir to stay the sweet winemaking region it's always been? It would be easy to attribute a single reason for Bettane's dislike. But in reality, neither life nor wine is so simple. And questioning certain attitudes, no matter who voices them, keeps us all honest.

The Dirt

The whole big wedge of schist in the Loire (discussed in the Muscadet chapter, page 88) started out as sediments 540 million years ago before they evolved from shale by the erection of that enormous mountain range, the Hercynian. Each time the mountains pushed forth, they thrust up the crest, heating and compressing rocks on the gigantic foothills. From there, the shale metamorphed into types of schists.

The Loire River, the longest in France, the one that meanders and breaks into tributaries and links all of the regions, became a dividing line between the white and the black soils. Both regions were linked by south-facing slopes of slate and schist between the Loire, Aubance, and Layon Rivers. Mingled into the soil is also *schistes gréseux*—clayish schist with some silica, sometimes called sandy shale—a mongrel clay made up of plenty of quartz, mica, and feldspar. Additionally, there are bits of igneous rocks, green basaltic spilite, and greenish rhyolite, prevalent in that village famous for Chenin, Savennières.

The Grapes

The Touraine poet Rabelais mentioned Chenin Blanc, previously known as Plant d'Anjou, in 1534 in the first book of his *Gargantua*.

But, as wonderful as it is, the grape has issues. It buds early and ripens late, which in the northern Loire is a very inconvenient truth. This means it's vulnerable to late frosts, which kill the bud or flower, as well as the rains during harvest time. But what doesn't kill you makes you stronger.

Pascaline, a great Chenin supporter and defender, explained: "There's no other grape that is so responsive to soil or its farmer. If you don't know what you're doing, you'll make crap wine. But it has a lot of natural characteristics that make it great: acidity, the tannin from its skins, a rhubarb, savory aspect to the fruit. It can be made in any style, from sparkling to sweet. And it is semi-aromatic. I just don't love really aromatic grapes. Semi-aromatic ones express so much more as they are more transparent to their terroir."

This grape gets around. At one time, it was the most widely planted vine in California. Now there's barely a thimbleful of Chenin plantings in the Golden State, having shrunk to a mere 5,000 acres or so. Yet new plantings abound, and those hunting down the remaining old vines are finding a renaissance, mostly on sand or loam. South Africa has more

Chenin acreage than the Loire. It was once called Steen. But there, too, it was either used as a blending grape or yanked out and Chardonnay was plunked in. In truth, much of their Chenin was awful, but the only ones to blame were the winemakers. There, as in California, it's making a comeback.

Anjou and slate soils aren't home to white alone. There are reds here as well. Do look for Grolleau, a much maligned grape that managed to get the reputation of only being good for the garbage. That slander only came about because it had been abused in the vineyard. In the hands of Joël Ménard (Domaine des Sablonnettes) and Benoit Courault, you'll be happy if you like a high-acid velvet wine. But the king to Chenin's queen is Cabernet Franc. On the schist of the Noir, you'll find more concentration and power, and perhaps a bit more of what is called "rustic."

Winemaker Profile: Richard Leroy

The schist-rich Rablay-sur-Layon and surroundings were once famed for their sweet wines, but now they're getting invaded by natural winemakers who want to make dry ones. We visited one of these new iconoclasts, the schist Chenin master Richard Leroy.

Leroy, a soccer player-turned investment banker-turned-vigneron, was influenced by the no-sulfur, natural winemaking of Domaine des Sablonnettes and Mark Angeli. Today, Richard Leroy makes only dry white wines. And he makes only two cuvées, from two distinct vineyards. His wines are celebrated and have found their way into the cellars of collectors and onto fancy wine lists. Yet in 2010, after experimenting for five years, he ditched safety and went sulfur-free. This was to be our first taste.

When Leroy opened his door to us, we saw a lunch party in

motion, with an assorted crew including winemaker Benoit Courault and the (then) furry Leroy himself, who immediately splashed wine into our glasses. This wine had been pulled from his private cellar. It was a leftover from the days when he had a fancy job and more conventional tastes. Drumroll, please: it was a 1989 Coche-Dury Les Rougeots. Many of our friends who collect the stuff would be plotzing at our good fortune. Today it was worth about $700.

"What do you think?" Richard asked.

For us, this famous wine was a disaster: short, acrid, and generally inexpressive. The others nodded in agreement. Leroy commented how his tastes had changed over the years, as he evolved from a trophy collector to a seeker of sincere wines. I had to note the dichotomy: poison to us was another's pleasure. We let the trophy bottle sit in its loneliness. Pascaline and I reached for Richard's 2012.

Labeling his two single-vineyard wines as Vin de France, Leroy left the appellation of Anjou for good in 2008. He has the luxury of name recognition. His customers are buying Richard Leroy and not Anjou. Like so many others there, he believes that's worth more to him than a classification that he thinks has no standards of quality. His wines, though both from the black soils, are wonderful in a side-by-side comparison, with exactly the same vinification. The fact that both had undergone malo allowed us to compare the soil's impact, in this case the more volcanic rhyolite versus the more metamorphic schist.

The Clos des Rouliers is a small parcel, all 0.7 hectares close to the Layon River. It is gray schist with some gravel texture. Pascaline saw the resulting wine as broader, with more aromatics up front and flavors of root vegetable, flower, and white tea. I saw it as an extrovert, with plenty of savory fruit and high-toned leather on the finish. Rich, with the creaminess of a Meursault and 13.5% ABV, it needs to shed the baby fat to be a stunner.

Les Noëls de Montbenault came from a rockier hilltop site, where it's windier and the 50-year-old vines grow on metamorphosed *schistes gréseux* with bands of igneous, volcanic rhyolite. We admit to a preference for the wines out of this 2-hectare vineyard. There was some reduction, but after that came violet. It was more refined, less overtly sexy, more angular, with a vibrant finish.

Richard's Chenins have made it onto some of the most exciting wine lists, whether natural or not, in the world. When we ask him about the nature of terroir, he says, "Terroir wines are produced by people who understand their soils. Soils are to be navigated, whether there is the roundness from the sandy shale or the power from the volcanic and the schist." In other words, you can abuse terroir and make a stupid wine anywhere, but to make a wine of depth you have to commune with the soil and listen to its needs—much like any good relationship.

Noir and Blanc Chenin Cheat Sheet

ANJOU NOIR

1. Appellations for Dry Wines: Anjou, Savennieres, Savennieres-Roche aux Moines, Savennieres-Coulee de Serrant
   Appellations for Sweet Wines: Beaulieu-sur-Layon, Faye-

d'Anjou, Rablay-sur-Layon, Rochefort-sur-Loire, Saint-Aubin-de-Luigné, Saint-Lambert-du-Lattay, Chaume, Quarts-de-Chaume, Bonnezeaux, Coteaux de l'Aubance, Anjou Coteaux de la Loire

2. Soils: green and purple schists, *schistes gréseux*, slate, volcanic (rhyolite, spilite, etc.)
3. Influences: Atlantic influence with a warmer, drier microclimate; humidity from rivers
4. Historically warmer shallow cellars near street level (as the harder stone makes digging deep cellars impossible)
5. Will go through partial to full malolactic fermentation
6. More affected by *Botrytis*
7. Profile: lusher, fuller, higher in alcohol, more dry extract, can be varietal if not farmed properly

ANJOU BLANC

1. Appellations for Anjou Blanc: Samur. While the towns of Puy-Notre-Dame, Champigny, and Brézé are not recognized as Cru for the whites, there are some fantastic wines coming from them. You should definitely seek out the Chenins from this area.
2. Soils: limestone (including yellow and white tuffeau), flint in Puy-Notre-Dame
3. Influences: More continental, drier, and less humid wind
4. Due to softer soil, easier to dig deep for deeper and colder cellars
5. Malo: often none
6. Profile: There are some sweet wines, but this place is more famous for dry and semi-sweet wines; the dry wines are more angular, lemony, and structured

WHO TO DRINK

- Ferme de la Sansonnière/Mark Angeli (biodynamic)
- Richard Leroy (biodynamic)
- Benoît Courault (organic)
- Kenji & Mai Hodgson (organic)
- Didier Chaffardon (organic)
- Domaine des Sablonnettes (organic)
- Domaine Patrick Baudouin (organic)
- Pithon-Paillé (organic)
- Les Vignes Herbel (organic)
- Les Vignes de Babass (organic)
- Jean-Christophe Garnier (organic)
- Agnès & René Mosse (organic)
- Toby Bainbridge (organic)
- Domaine Les Grandes Vignes (biodynamic)
- Jean-François Chéné (organic)
- Olivier Cousin (organic)
- Stéphane Bernaudeau (biodynamic)
- Domaine de Bablut (organic)
- Bruno Rochard (organic)
- La Grange aux Belles (organic)
- Sébastien Fleuret (organic)
- Philippe Delmée & Aurélien Martin (organic)
- Damien Bureau (organic)

Savennières

On the north bank of the Loire, on hills of schist facing southwest and opening up on to the river, lies this nearly 363-acre appellation. There are some other grapes planted here but its best to think of this area as 100 percent beautiful Chenin. It's tucked into a tiny hamlet and has been known since Roman times for its extraordinary wine. "Legendary" is the word that comes to mind. It's been said that it is here where Chenin blanc rises to the same stature as Burgundy's Montrachet. Well, never mind that it is only in recent memory, as late as the 1960s, that these wines were made in a dry style. But what they are on that schist is intense, powerful, and sometimes quite high in alcohol. No matter what the potential, Savennières was resting on its heritage, with few people working the soil and letting the land speak—that is, until Nicolas Joly rolled into town and changed everything.

I had been told not to worry about the interview. All I needed to do was say hello, sit down, and Nicolas Joly, the leader of one of the most powerful movements in viticulture, biodynamics, would proceed to talk. I introduced myself. In the midst of a chaos of stacked paper, I sat on a plump, chintz-covered couch as he asked to the air: "Where to start?" He didn't wait for an answer before he began chattering about biodynamics, his Return to Terroir tasting series, and the current crisis in the wine world. He may be a little nuts, but any visionary is.

Nicolas Joly, born in 1945, is a former banker who escaped New York and London. He ran back to the banks of the Loire, to his family's estate, said to be one of the most profound sites for Chenin Blanc in the world, Coulée de Serrant in the hamlet of Savennières.

The estate's vineyard, its own appellation and a *monopole*, was planted in 1130 by the Cistercians and appeals to mystics and gourmands alike. The reputation of the wines goes back almost as long and was noted by Louis XI, who referred to them as the "gold drop." For centuries, they were considered among the finest wines of France. The grape, of course, was one factor. Chenin Blanc does something special on those complex and historic soils, mainly schist, with some patches of volcanic. The vineyard Coulée de Serrant is the spiritual heart of the domaine and overlooks the Loire River. In addition, Joly (increasingly joined by his daughter Virginie) works other parcels, including Les Vieux Clos just below Coulée in the Savennières AOC, and Le Clos de la Bergerie tucked in the appellation of La Roche aux Moines.

Joly returned there in 1977 and found that the vines had fallen into disgrace. He soon came across a book by Rudolf Steiner, the Austrian philosopher. It was a copy of his 1921 lectures that became the basis for biodynamic farming. By 1984, Joly's entire vineyards had been converted to working biodynamically. At that point, he was well on his way to becoming a hero to some and a crackpot to others. I'm in the hero camp.

I sat there that afternoon mesmerized. My friend was right. I didn't have to say a thing as he channeled various mystical wisdoms. He was enthralling. His tasting road show Renaissance des Appellations, or Return to Terroir, was bursting at the seams with new blood. He was thrilled. "The new biodynamic enthusiast is like a young dog hunting on the first day," Joly said. "This new generation is fabulous. They were made for biodynamics."

Today, the region is a hotbed of biodynamic viticulture, with people timing their treatments to the moon and wanting to taste wines on a fruit or flower day instead of a root or leaf. No matter what you believe, the wines farmed this way are among the finest. To quote Joly on the value of the scientific minutiae:

"Look, as a farmer you need water. How does it help you to know that water is H_2O?"

WHO TO DRINK

- Vignobles de la Coulée-de-Serrant (biodynamic)
- Loïc Mahé (organic)
- Eric Morgat (organic)

- Domaine du Closel/Evelyne de Jessey (biodynamic)
- Domaine aux Moines/Tessa Laroche (biodynamic)
- Clément Baraut (biodynamic)
- Thibaud Boudignon (organic)
- Damien Laureau (biodynamic)
- Patrick Baudouin (organic)
- Agnès & René Mosse (biodynamic)
- Pithon-Paillé (organic)

The Languedoc-Roussillon

The large area of Languedoc-Roussillon stretches from the western border of the Rhône to the Spanish border of Catalonia. It's circled by the Massif Central and the Pyrénées Mountains and embraced on its southern coast by the Mediterranean Sea.

Even though it's blessed with limestone (such as parts of the well-known regions of Pic Saint-Loup, Saint-Jean-de-Minervois, and especially in Corbières) and whatever other soils the globe can dream up, on the craggy vistas and wind-battered hills it is the metamorhpic that is the foundation for much of this area's identity.

Ever since the Romans, the secret's been out that if you find flat, boring lands, it's almost too easy to grow grapes there. Thus began a regrettable reputation that has been difficult to overcome. Plonky brands like Fat Bastard became Languedoc-Roussillon's calling card. In the '90s, this brand became one of the leaders in the Fighting Varietals movement. Their bottles boldly put Pinot Noir or Syrah on the label instead of the place. This was heartbreaking, because in that land existed villages of such talent! Inside the Languedoc, up on the hills and cliffs, were appellations like Faugères and Saint-Chinian. In the Roussillon, there was Maury, Fitou, Collioure, and Banyuls. They had an abundance of old vines, whipped into miniature bushes they call gobelets by the punishing winds and the infertile schistous soils, but which gave balanced wines of character. Tragically, they went begging because of the ensuing lack of respect.

To super-simplify their schist story, it's not dissimilar from the Anjou Noir's, just more recent. Sediment from Paleozoic Era mud, clay, quartz, and fossils changed to schist and some moved on to gneiss. Because of the development of the Pyrénées, the best soils also have altitude and proximity to the sea. The result is a profound amount of very complex soils, with a dominance of schists that is more or less decomposed, gneiss, and even in some patches sedimentary-derived, limestone-based soils.

Faugères and Saint-Chinian are on the foothills on the Black Mountains (Montagne Noire) between 600 and 1,500 feet. Banyuls and Collioure seem to plunge directly from the Alberes and Pyrenees mountains to the Mediterranean Sea. Maury is at 1,200 feet. These altitudes are excellent for giving the vine what it needs, especially in hot areas: cooler nights in order to retain freshness.

Schists are particularly great when they sit at a right angle to the Earth. That way, the roots can go deep down and find water, alleviating what the vine pros call hydric stress (when the plant shuts down because it is too hot and warm, which can lead to green, unripe tannins and aromas), and if they also have a little clay mixed with limestone marl, even better. Given the heat-retaining power of schist, this is essential for important regions, as the slow ripening, without cooking, goes on through the dark hours.

Faugères

Faugères as an accepted wine-growing region came into its own rather late, around the time of the French Revolution. Nearly two centuries later, it was given its appellation status in 1982. Yet, its terroir of significant schist is so very noteworthy. It shows up in three forms. The large slabs are called *dalles*. Hardly anything grows on that soil, except the vine, and the yields are super-low. Another less mean kind of soil is *schistes gréseux* because of its more clay-like texture. The friable, very brittle, fragile type which you can break in your fingers is called *frites*. With constant erosion from the wind and the sun, the rock breaks down in the most lovely ways, making it easy to feed the vine the necessary nutrients.

Many people here have a special relationship to their soil, such as Corinne Andrieu from Clos Fantine. "I think that schist radiates an energy that has an effect on the behavior of man," she wrote to us.

Talk to different growers and you'll get different ideas. But Pascaline and I are giving our votes to Grenache and Carignan. Carignan needs long, slow growth to be gorgeous. The Grenache needs to struggle so it doesn't create wines of such high alcohol you'll need an ice cube to drink it. But when all of these conditions are working together, the results can be spectacular. This area is spectacular for value.

WHO TO DRINK

- Clos Fantine; Faugères (organic)
- Frédéric Brouca; Faugères (organic)
- Léon Barral; Faugères (biodynamic)
- Mas d'Alezon; Faugères (organic)
- Domaine Jean-Michel Alquier; Faugères (sustainable)
- Domaine Bordes; Saint Chinian (organic)
- Yannick Pelletier; Saint Chinian (organic)
- Domaine Canet-Valette; Saint Chinian (organic)

Banyuls and Collioure

It would be a pity not to mention the southwestern lands of Collioure and Banyuls. Small and little-known, they're more famous for their picture-postcard harbors and delicious anchovies. They're also marked by thousands of schist terraces sculpting the black cliffs that seem to fall right into the sapphire-blue of the Mediterranean. This is the beauty of contrast, and you can see it in their wines. Historically, under the name Banyuls, they were fortified, a technique developed during the 13th century, where some alcohol is added during the fermentation of the grape in order to balance and preserve a wine. On the black, poor slopes, the hand-pruned Grenache, king of the appellation in the three colors, yields little and concentrates intensely, getting just a little freshness from the sea. Only fortification and a long aging, in demi-john glass or cask, could tame such a beast of sugar, tannins, and alcohol to reveal after years bottles that can compete with that other fortified schist hero, port. Recently, because of the lack of market love for these wines and the improvement of chilling techniques, more dry vintages are being made, most still on the overripe and monotone side. But don't let this fool you. There are gems among the rough.

WHO TO DRINK

- Domaine La Tour Vieille; Collioure (sustainable)
- Domaine du Traginer/Jean-Francois Deu; Collioure (biodynamic)
- La Petite Baigneuse; Banyuls (organic)
- Alain Castex (previously Le Casot des Mailloles); Banyuls (biodynamic)
- Bruno Duchêne; Banyuls (organic)

Galicia's Slate Zone

If France's Anjou Noir had a twin region, it would be on the northwestern shores of Spain's Galicia. Both regions border the Atlantic and are capable of producing wines of such very pretty transparency, wines that are gulpable yet never cease to satisfy.

Both the Loire and Ribeira Sacra start with granite near the coast.

And while there are still a lot of granitic outposts, as you inch inland you encounter a lot of schist and slate. But where in the Loire, the search for schist leads you to the relatively flat land of Anjou, a search for metamorphic rocks in this part of Spain leads you through twisty roads into mountainous Galicia and the magic kingdom of Ribeira Sacra.

Ribeira Sacra

Sacred River is the meaning of Ribeira Sacra, and it refers to the point where the Miño and Sil rivers converge. It gets its name from early Christian times, when holy sites and monasteries proliferated on the nearby pilgrimage path of Camino de Santiago. It's profoundly wine country, with vineyards rising up dramatically over both rivers. Those of the Sil are steeper, rockier, and more inaccessible than the greener, gentler banks of the Miño.

Getting there is quite the experience. Arrive by plane into Vigo, stop at the wine bar Bagos in Pontevedra, taste Albariño in Rías Baixas, then drive inland, past Ourense. That's when the drive gets complicated with twisty hairpin turns up the mountains. Carsickness invariably results. Finally, the doors slam, and out into the air, there's relief! Scramble up to the stone-walled, terraced vineyards, and then stand in awe.

Follow that prescription, and I promise, the full effect of this area's beauty will stun you. Ribeira Sacra might be one of the top places for breathtaking vineyards in the world. Because of the steep incline of the vineyards that dive down treacherously to the river, more than one person tumbles to their death during the harvest every year. The land is not only beautiful but talented, so it is shocking that it only was granted DO status in 1996.

We were in the region of Amandi with winemaker Roberto Santana. Originally from the Canary Islands (see Igneous chapter on page 60), he and three other friends from enology school created their collective winery called Envínate. The friends banded together to explore winemaking where the Atlantic Ocean has influence. They want to make, as they call them, Vinos Atlánticos. They found people who were working organically, or at least open to organic growing, where there were old vines and a history.

For their Ribeira experiment, they found three plots of earth, including a spot in slate-heavy dirt, punctuated with the pink quartzes and granite of Amandi. The draw was the temperate climate, with less rain than on the coast, and the potential for ripening red grapes was terrific.

Santana popped open a bottle from that very vineyard, the Parcela Seoane. One hundred percent whole-grape cluster fermentation deepens the savory elements. As we sipped it, we found it rich, for sure, fleshy but with a rusty kind of core that some call minerality. Happily, in silence I contemplated the plunging neckline of the slope, which dissolved into the Sil River below.

"You have to be crazy to work here," I said to myself as I looked at Santana, thinking of the kind of glorious passion he and others have to have to rebuild the broken wall terraces, revitalize the soil, and either live here or commute to this rural, isolated—if beautiful—part of the world.

Across the other bank and the mountain that rose off of it, through the early spring trees, we could see the ghosts of the past: terraces from centuries past that had been abandoned long ago. I thought of all the tales of these forests being populated by witches, faeries, and ghosts, and at that moment I could almost see them for myself. So fogged over, even though the weather was not at all foggy, it was as if the image was shrouded in Vaseline.

The Dirt

Those vineyards are in the mountain range that is part of the Galician Massif, formed during the collision of the Iberian Plate and a fragment of crust from another continent called the Meguma Terrane—a piece of earth that was all the way over in the Atlantic, near Nova Scotia. In the process, shale, under high temperatures and pressure, turned into slate and schist. According to geologist Alex Maltman, "Slate is an aggregate of several complex silicate minerals bonded to give a characteristic aptitude for cleaving into thin sheets. It is palpably absurd that somehow in the wine there exists a cleavable, complex solid."

Maltman is one of many in the science world engaged in this heated argument against soil having an impact on taste, and he likes to talk of "minerality" in the wine. But as we were all standing in Amandi, drinking wine that was so precise and fresh and crunchy, there was no doubt that the slate and the grape were a heaven-made match. Funny, what is good in slate for the Mencía is also good for roofing materials: the low tendency to absorb water, which makes it useful in a wet climate, and its ability to warm up the earth and retain the heat. It works well in high elevations where the temperature drops in the darkness of night. In the Priorat, this certainly helps tease the wines into outrageously high alcohols, often near 16 percent. But there they have gone to mostly Grenache-based wines, and Grenache, as a grape, loves to manufacture alcohol.

Slate crumbles easily, so if the soil is properly worked (and that is essential, as always) the vine root squiggles its pathways through inhospitable soils. Some writers I've read say that they've been told that the slate gives a spine to reds, with black stone or moist cellar floor flavors. But that might be leaning too heavily on a romantic notion of direct traceability. The real effect the soil has is in how well it affords the vine access to what it needs in order to be in balance. In snooping through ancient books I came across this intriguing quote in a 19-century book called *A Helping Hand for Town and Country*: "The principal potash minerals are feldspar and mica, and these are mainly contained in granite, gneiss, and mica slate. Soils, therefore, that are derived in a good measure from these rocks are the richest in potash and therefore, other things being equal, the best for vineyards." That might be one of the reasons that slate and granite—two big favorites for soil—do so well.

Atlantic Wines: The Power of Water

There's always another word-of-the-moment making the rounds among the wine set. Sexy? So very 2009. But what does sexy in a wine actually mean? It's different things to different people, so let's just go with the G-rated definition: seductive. Then there was the word crunchy. That one circled around France for a couple of years, then touched down in New York City more recently. It makes sense if you imagine a textural sense of snap, acid, and bite, a sense of structure just before you break through the ice. But if you want to stay ahead of the game, prime yourself for Atlantic wines.

These are wines that fall under the powerful influence of the Atlantic. Large bodies of water can moderate coastal climates, making for less extreme seasonal variations than seen inland. You may be more familiar with the sunny, relatively rain-free joys of the Mediterranean climate, but what about the Atlantic? It's the Earth's second largest body of water, and along with the Pacific it ties for the world's saltiest ocean. Most (though not all, climate is never a simple thing) northwest Atlantic climes are cloudy and rainy and generally mild, which means longer growing seasons. With winds out of the west, these areas are humid. Get out your map and you'll see a loose group emerge: Long Island, the western coastal Loire, Galicia, the northern side of Tenerife, Rías Baixas, Jerez, parts of Portugal such as Colares and the Minho province (great for Vinho Verde), Maine, Prince Edward Island, and Nova Scotia (hello, climate change!), and, of course, western Bordeaux.

So what does "Atlantic" feel like . . . or really, taste like? What you can count on are refreshing wines with salinity, acidity, and natural grace. They're lower in alcohol, yet ripe. The fruit can be touched by seaweed and black tea. The wines can be vivacious and something called crunchy, like the snap you get biting into a fruit. White or red, they refresh.

The Grapes

The rules for Ribeira Sacra permit about 21 grape varieties. But permitting isn't the same as preferring. My advice is to forget it and just go for the best growers and drink whatever they plant. The whites are planted mostly on granite. The ones you need to remember are Godello, Loureiro, and Treixadura, all underrated. Palomino, the grape of Jerez, was at one point the most widely planted grape, but is it the best suited to this location? I'm not so sure. Among the reds allowed are Brancellao, Sousón, Garnacha, Tintorera (aka Alicante Bouchet) Merenzao (also known as Trousseau and Bastardo), Caiño Tinto, and some Tempranillo.

What are considered the minor grapes, Espadeiro and Caiño Tinto are forgotten greats. They remind me so much of my beloved Gamay. However, Mencía is the regional star, making up about 85 percent of the vines, although it does have some issues. Being of fragile skin, it's susceptible to *Botrytis* and mildew. Being a low-acid grape, it absolutely must be picked quickly when ready so it doesn't lose its edge. Contrary to past belief, the grape has no relation to Cabernet Franc. Adding stems, as with Cabernet Franc, can be tricky but more and more people are experimenting with using the whole cluster. It is often extremely raspberry-like and redcurranty, and when it falls below 13 percent alcohol, it shines its absolute best.

Winemaker Profile: Laura Lorenzo, Daterra Viticultores

A gorgeous woman with dreadlocks down to her waist, Laura Lorenzo is ready to take on the wine world. "I'm offended by vines on a wire. It's slavery," she said, standing over her little dwarfed vine. Then she began to giggle, suddenly self-conscious about the way she must sound. I thought she sounded terrific.

No one has seen a woman like this in the vines near Galicia's rural Manzaneda, where she lives. There it's a mixture of peasants who have forsaken the vines or newcomers with enthusiasm and deep pockets. But for a local woman and first-generation wine-maker to be doing all this heavy lifting herself? I'm not sure the locals are ready for her. Maybe that's why all of her farm equipment was stolen in her first year. But her way of dealing with it is remarkably proud: "I may be poor, but I have hands."

Laura came from the city of Ourense. While only about 40 minutes away, it seems like the other side of the Earth in terms of population and accessibility. These days, Laura lives in a remote ancient village and works to reclaim land that was long ago forsaken. But she did get some experience at the beginning in the big leagues with a large winery named Dominio do Bibei before she finally got the nerve to strike out on her own, which is rare enough in this area, let alone if you're a woman. Along the way, people have helped her in huge ways. They've donated space for her to vinify. Others gave her land just in exchange for her bringing it back to life after decades of chemical abuse. Her parcels are split up into different regions, one amid the wild thyme and more fragile old granite soils. She is not in Amandi, but is just about an hour away from Roberto of Envínate and Pedro Rodríquez from Guímaro, as the car drives. She works on five different parcels. While this area, like Faugères, is famed for its schist, it's not all that simple. The soils are siliceous, she said, which is similar to the *schistes grèseux* of Faugères, a highly acidic schist soil mixed with clay that has very fine heat retention properties. And it is also a place where the granite and slate coexist. This is why she's in a good position to consider them both. She explained that the Ribeira Sacra speaks to both worlds. The granite gives a more Atlantic influence and the slate brings a more Mediterranean feel. In hot years, the granite gives freshness, while in cold years the slate brings warmth.

Through working with quite a few different kinds of terroirs in Ribeira Sacra and nearby Valdeorras, she's found that the differences between granitic soils and clay or slate (normally slate soils have more clay) is that the temperature of granite changes faster. Also, in rain, granitic soil drains more quickly than slate. Slate holds more water. But many of these qualities can be tempered, depending on how you work the soil and nourish the organisms that live in it. And that is why she's reclaiming soils, moving toward organic and her version of biodynamics. Everything seems possible. And from sipping her wines, it is obviously working.

Lorenzo's very first wine released was the Gavela Blanco. It's made from Palomino, a grape frequently found in sherry. While the grape is often dismissed, she has made a lovely wine with it. I found it to be lemony, sandy, and very strongly Atlantic—you could taste the sea breeze. Her other white offering, Erea de Vila Blanco, is a field blend dominated by Godello with bits of Treixadura, Albariño, and Doña Blanca. This had notes of melon and juice, with a less sandy texture.

Winemaker Profile: Pedro of Adegas Guímaro

Pedro Rodríguez held a long skinny knife in front of me. With a huge smile, he said, "This is what I use to kill the pig." Everyone else was amused by this, but as a vegetarian, I knew he was just teasing me. This impish man, always laughing and teasing, has almost rebuilt each wall of his terrace himself. Does he ever stop beaming? His enthusiasm is generous, and so are his wines. Before 1991, Pedro's family made small quantities of wine for their own consumption and sold their wine in *garrafones* (20-liter glass containers) to local cantinas. But in 1996, Pedro Rodríguez led his family into a new world. Amandi is his territory. Pedro has also started a massive project of working organically, planting heirloom grape varieties at the highest elevations in his subregion. When standing in the vines, in the expansive amphitheater of terraces so close to Roberto's vineyard, it seemed like an entirely different place. But the work in the winery is similar: wild yeast fermentation, foot treading in open-top vessels, the use of stems, working with low sulfur, and no new oak. This is the recipe the most talented are using to find the best in their wines. Some of his wines to look for: Guímaro Tinto is all in stainless steel and is 100 percent joy. Then there's Finca Meixemán, from a single 1.2-hectare plot of 70-year-old Mencía vines planted on schist at 400-450 meters. His Finca Capeliños comes from a plot of almost 90-year-old vines. You'll find a deeper expression from these older vines. These single-vineyard plots are wines to put down for at least ten years, though you can certainly enjoy them now.

- Luis Rodíguez; Ribeiro (sustainable)
- Envínate "Lousas"; Ribeira Sacra (organic)
- Laura Lorenzo; Ribeira Sacra (organic)
- Pedro Rodríguez; Ribeira Sacra (organic)
- Bernardo Estevez; Ribeiro (biodynamic)
- Nacho Gonzalez; Valdeorras (organic)

The Mosel

Willkommen to Germany and particularly the Mosel. The region used to be called the Mosel-Saar-Ruwer, which cited the two tributaries of its main river, but nowadays, it's just Mosel. This is Germany's only region that is famous for slate and schist. Mosel took a long time to establish a reputation but a short time to undo it. Blame Blue Nun and Liebfraumilch, the Yellow Tails of their time. Sweet, crappy wines, they obscured all of the wonderful wines of Germany, and it took decades for people to start to come back to the complexity of their most famed grape, Riesling.

In the northwest part of Germany, the Mosel River snakes through the winegrowing region. The steep slopes (and we're talking stratospheric) rise from the riverbed, and all along are picturesque towns that seem like gingerbread cartoons. It's a pretty region that has had hard knocks aside from the commercial wines. There was terrible chemical farming, removing acid, back sweetening, and other obscenities, not to say anything about those difficult labels. German wine labels are about the most difficult to decipher. But to hell with that. Just hunt out the right producers and go on their ride. You'll enter a fascinating arena of long-lived white wines of great complexity and joy. You love dry wines? They're here. Sweet? Well, few regions do it better. The region is famed for fierce acidity and its extreme climate—wet and chilly, with a mean temperature of about 65 degrees Fahrenheit in the summer—ridiculously steep slopes (the steepest in the world, also about 65 degrees) and above all else, slate and schist and more slate and schist. You can find both in the vineyard, even though everyone calls it all slate, or *schiefer*.

The Dirt

When we talk about the Mosel, we mostly talk about the Middle Mosel. With its many colors of slate, warmed by the microclimates of the rivers and pestered by wet, cool weather, making wine there is not easy. When I was last there in 2007, oh, my, did it rain! I could barely see the famed slate, as the terroir was obscured by a carpet of giant brown slugs. I still have nightmares of the squish and slip under my shoes as I tried not to slide down the steep incline into the river. But the wine is undeniably good. This is just one of the made-in-heaven combinations of severe winter, sunless summers, and a vine matched to its savior soil. Here, it seems like Riesling is almost indestructible. Here, the slate acts as a much-needed plant warmer, holding on to the marginal rays of sun and draining the soil so it doesn't get waterlogged. But remembering that slug-riddled soil, I had to wonder, was it organic? Unlikely. So few were back then, and there are still so few organic producers right now, as you can see from the list of preferred winemakers below. One clue was that the earth was closed up and compacted, such that it couldn't drain.

Drainage is essential in wet weather, especially in Mosel, where the topsoil is thin. Beneath it is pure broken slate. This one rock comes in three main colors: gray, blue, and red. With that also come three different colors of soil. Many claim that the different colors of soil create very different wines. Clemens Busch is one such man. A biodynamic grower in the Mosel, he says that "the gray gives a more elegant style, a softer slate with yellow fruits and white peach." The blue Devonian slate, Busch says, gives intense astringency when young but in its finish explodes with yellow fruit that's more ripe, exotic, and tropical. Red slate gets its color from high iron content and delivers more herbal notes plus more structure and complexity, but the vines need about seven years to develop.

The Grapes

There may be a few minor grapes here that so far have not distinguished themselves, such as Müller-Thurgau and Kerner. Those also creep into the north of Italy. There's a little of that more interesting Auxerrois and Weissburgunder that you also find in Alsace. And there is a touch of red. That's their Spätburgunder, more well known to us as Pinot noir. But usually the Pinot is over in the warmer regions like Baden on sediments—here we are talking mostly about white wine and Riesling.

The Riesling grape is said to have originated in the Rheingau, about a 45-minute drive from Mosel toward Frankfurt. The vine has hard wood, so it stands up to a solid frost. Because it is late ripening, it is great for climates with late growing seasons. It is not that susceptible to rot, which makes it great for Germany's soft, soggy weather, and also means it can be left hanging longer on the vine to be picked riper and can handle the noble rot. Thanks to the fact that people are growing better grapes, as well as an increased need for dryness, the country has segued to making much more dry Riesling. But the high acid content also makes it perfect for sweet wines because they never tire with that beautiful spark. Other regions that do well with Riesling but do not have the same slate soils are the sunnier and warmer Austria and the Alsatian section of France. It is linked to Australia too, with some legendary Rieslings made in the Clare Valley, where there is a mix of red clay, limestone, and slate soils. When the producers get their act together—which seems to be happening right now—it's showing nicely on the shale soils of the Finger Lakes of New York State.

- Weingut Clemens Busch (biodynamic)
- Weingut Immich-Batterieberg (organic)
- Rita and Rudolf Trossen (biodynamic)
- Hofgut Falkenstein (sustainable)
- Weiser-Künstler (organic)
- Weingut Florian Lauer (sustainable)
- Weingut Knebel (sustainable)
- Weingut Ulrich Stein (sustainable)
- Weingut Vollenweider (sustainable)
- Weingut Egon Müller (sustainable)

GNEISS

With lively colored lines of sediment running through it, gneiss looks like granite, but it is fully metamorphic. The rock makes for a relatively infertile soil, and if you proceed on the wisdom that what is good for grapes is not good for corn, we have a winner. Certainly we have evidence in the wines of Cyril Fahl, who works in the Roussillon, or Guy Bossard, who championed bottling his gneiss terroir as a single-rock Muscadet. The banded rock is also part of the vineyard foundation that Austria refers to as its beloved primary rock. Gneiss shows up in the muscular region of Wachau, making intense wines on dramatic rocky slopes with very little topsoil, such as those of Nikolaihoff, west of Vienna. And quite close, in the Kamptal, Martin Arndorfer makes wine from some of the most esteemed terroir in Austria, Heiligenstein.

Austria and the Kamptal

Oddly enough, in a country so keen on serious biodynamic and organic food, the progess for wine has been lagging in Austria. Additionally, there's a hell of a lot of irrigation, in some places perhaps needed as the vines are planted right on the rock. But in other places, it's merely a convenience. While there are lots of seriously natural people working in Styria, closer to Slovenia, and not far from Vienna, there's a new generation coming. Many of the soils in Lower Austria are sedimentary, windblown loess. People like Christian Tschida are doing remarkable work there. But much of that weird soil is located just 40 minutes west of the big city in the Kamptal region, which gets its name from the Kamp River. In Austria, gneiss is revered.

Winemaker Profile: Martin Arndorfer

Kamptal is home to four different terroirs, textures, and bedrocks: sandstone, loess, gravel, and gneiss. The gneiss is the one that provokes reverence. And if you get to taste some wine from the Arndorfer Estate, you'll find out why.

Martin Arndorfer makes wine with his wife Anna Steininger. Together, they have generations of family wine behind them. In 2009, they started to move toward organic methods and minimal intervention. They're an adorable, lively couple. Martin has bedhead hair and almost goofy enthusiasm. Anna is a bit more grounded, and together they're incredible, always experimenting. For example, they have this totally delicious rosé of Zweigelt made on the skins, along with a small percentage of skins of Grüner Veltliner in order to bring more structure to a fun rosé.

They make wines from Grüner Veltliner, Riesling, Neuburger, Chardonnay and Zweigelt, all grown mostly on sedimentary loess and gravel. But Arndorfer and Steininger do also have gneiss-derived soils. Arndorfer told me that his vines never get tired of it. Even in the dry summers, the vine can never deplete that soil. But there is a problem: like granite, gneiss soil has no water retention. While that's brilliant in the wet Nantes area, in Austria many look to irrigation, saying that if they don't, they won't get fruit in every vintage. Arndorfer says that in a perfect world, gneiss gives a darker, more focused fruit. So in years when there's plenty of rain, the vintage report might say avoid them, but go to high elevation, to the sublime terroirs of Gaisberg and Heiligenstein, and whammo, you'll find a great vintage. When that happens, thank the gneiss.

The famous hill of Gaisberg has gneiss, and that's where their Neuburger and a rarity called Roter Veltliner (no relation to Grüner Veltliner) come from. "These varieties can handle a low amount of water pretty well without losing quality or aromas," Arndorfer said. But not all grapes are so easygoing. "Grüner Veltliner, for example, is much more sensitive in water. If it gets water-stressed you can taste it, usually in a higher amount of phenolics and less focused fruit, kind of gray and dusty aromas," he says. "Riesling and Neuburger like gneiss. They usually can show a minerality and vibrancy, based on the minerality of gneiss, combined with a lively soil."

Arndorfer says that while his soil is said to be better for Riesling, he is growing Roter Veltliner. He might be the only one. Is it worth it? Oh, yes. It's a stunning, deep wine.

WHO TO DRINK

- Anna and Martin Arndorfer (sustainable)
- Jurtschitsch (organic)

- Weingut Loimer (biodynamic)
- Jo Landron, Les Houx (biodynamic)
- Vincent Caillé/Fay d'Homme, Terre de Gneiss, Fief Seigneur, Saint-Fiacre Oper Numero 7 (organic)
- Domaine de la Pépière, Monnières-Saint Fiacre (organic)
- Domaine l'Ecu, Gneiss (biodynamic)

AMPHIBOLITE

While my favorite of the Muscadet soils might be granitic, the majority is actually metamorphic: gneiss, orthogneiss, and amphibolite. The latter gives rise to the most iconic wine of the famously mustaschioed Jo Landron. But in a region that often bottles by soil, this one is usually left off the label. When I asked him, with a wink, he said, "It's a bad soil."

Landron created his wine and boldly called it Amphibolite as a challenge, trying to produce a more crystalline, salty Muscadet with a lower level of sulfite. Though it is viewed as a soil that cannot produce an age-worthy wine, if you score a bottle of Landron's Amphibolite you see that it ages just as beautifully as do his others, like Le Fief du Breil or Les Houx. "Maybe we could say that amphibolite is the sea-style of Muscadet," Landron mused. Fief du Breil on gneiss, then, would be the earthy side. "It's the yin and yang."

THE METAMORPHIC TASTING BOX

1. Jo Landron/Domaine de la Louvetrie, Amphibolite; Muscadet, Loire, France (amphibolite)

Melon always gives a neutral-smelling wine. This amphibolite, however, gives it more roundness in the mouth. The acids are certainly there, a

stoniness and angularity, but it's more quenching than mouthwatering. The aromatics are more open than on the granite, with a hint of elderflower and some seaweed brininess up front.

2. Richard Leroy, Les Rouliers; Vin de France/Anjou, Loire, France (schist)

Broad in the mouth, this Chenin washes over the tongue with long, fat strokes. The wine has some heft and substance. There's some root vegetable savory notes and hints of white tea. It's an extrovert, marked with more pomelo-like acid than lemon. A big personality and some leather-like tannin, but quality, fancy stuff on the finish. Here also is a pretty stunning bitterness specific to this place.

3. Immich-Batterieberg, Enkircher Eschburg Riesling; Mosel, Germany (slate)

There's some flesh in this Riesling, and some crunch as well. The acid is subtle, a little grapefruit, or is that kumquat? It creeps up on you and attacks. You'll feel it in the gums instead of in the mouth—and it holds on.

4. Martin and Anna Arndorfer, Von den Terrassen 1979; Kamptal, Austria (gneiss)

This wine is almost as aromatic as Riesling, but the edge of this rare grape, Roter Veltliner, and its siltiness sets it apart. A complex wine, with fleshy aromatic peach and a stick-to-itness ocean breeze. Stunning.

5. Guímaro, Tinto; Ribeira Sacra, Spain (slate)

Search for the aromatics in this Mencía. They are there, very peppery, with some black raspberry. Drink it, and you'll find them on the palate as well. But it's subtle, and underneath is a stoniness, a rock bed foundation.

There is a structure, but it's not very pronounced. It is not totally precise, but it's certainly very enjoyable.

6. Léon Barral, Faugères; Languedoc, France (schist)

The grapes here are Carignan, Grenache, and Cinsault. The herbs and the berry hit first. Then comes the solarity. The taste is warming. There's a mineral-like acid of iron and a little scratchy leather, but just a little, and just a touch of licorice and pepper. It is fat and oily, but then comes the structure of the skin tannins, and a very noble quinine-like bitterness to support the finish.

7. Cyril Fahl/Clos du Rouge Gorge, L'Ubac; Roussillon, France (gneiss)

L'Ubac refers to a slope with the least amount of sun and this is a crazy bottle, with a concentrated core and grippy acidity. It is dense, but at the same time lifted. Cherry skin and pith, reduced blueberry, tannic, grainy, and the taste goes on for quite a long time with an elegant chewiness. This is a blend: Cinsault, Grenache, and Carignan—with a very rare focus and an incredible freshness from this area.

Melon B, Chenin, Riesling, Mencía, Roter Veltliner, and Carignan (with some Grenache and Cinsault): what a phenomenal bunch of bedfellows! No one would ever put these together in a tasting unless you were looking for something rare and totally cool, like some primordial connection. Taste and compare. You know the drill. Things to note:

Acids: Are they more like a bitter orange (or kumquat)?

Tannins: Do the grapes seem to have a thicker skin and thus a white or green-tea-like quality? Are they more assertive?

Texture: Is there a certain austerity in the wines, a grainy, tannic feeling?

Structure: Does the wine seem bold, yet very lifted and dancing?

Metamorphic Cheat Sheet

Region	Bedrock	Climate	Known For
France: Loire, Anjou Noir	schist, slate	mild winters, warm summers; humid and western wind	Chenin, Cabernet Franc
France: Loire, Muscadet	gneiss, orthogneiss, amphibolite	plenty of rain in a mild climate, though winters can be cold and summers can have heat blasts	Melon
France: Languedoc, Faugères and Northeastern Saint-Chinian	schist	hot, dry summer with mild windy winters	Grenache, Carignan, Mourvèdre, Cinsault
France: Roussillon, Collioure and Banyuls	schist	wet, moderately cold winter, hot and dry summer	Carignan, Syrah, Macabeau
Spain: Priorat	llicorella (schist)	dry with extreme temperatures; hot and cold winds	Grenache, Carignan
Spain: Galicia, Ribeira Sacra	schist	long hot summers, cool autumns, plenty of rain	Brancellao, Treixadura Mencía, Godello
Germany: Mosel	schist, slate	cool summers with heat spikes, long autumns, cold winters; plenty of rain	Riesling
Austria: Kamptal, Wachau	gneiss	dry hot days, cool nights, long autumn	Riesling, Grüner, Veltliner, Roter Veltiner, Muskateller, Traminer

POSTSCRIPT: ALSACE STANDS ALONE

OVERVIEW OF ALSACE

In a very pure, brilliant, washed sunlight with an almost unnatural blue typical of Alsace, I picked up my car in Colmar and drove a mere half hour north toward a very atypical kind of vigneron. Patrick Meyer of Domaine Julien Meyer lives and farms in Nothalten. He makes a variety of whites, as Alsace is known for, especially Riesling, and a lovely Pinot Noir, the area's only approved red grape. It was in his Muenchberg vineyard that he told me with solemnity, "Some people have energy. It's the same with vineyards. Muenchberg is like this." Then, just a few hours later, the theme came up again when tasting among his barrels and egg-shaped cement fermenters. He saw a perplexed look on my face while trying to find the delicate rosewater of what I expected in that Riesling. Well, he'd have none of it, and started to insist, "It's Muenchberg! Not Riesling," he scolded, as if to say, *you idiot.*

Back in the day, around the same time the Burgundy monks were sussing out the prime plots, those in Alsace were hunting down the talented soils priming the best slopes, such as Hengst and Muenchberg. They discovered that there was a total mashup of bedrocks, and they considered them carefully. By the time the Middle Ages came about, Alsace was famous. But sharing northern and eastern borders with Germany was a problem. When yet again the Germans moved in on them in 1870, the invaders messed around with their vines. Because they had their own Riesling, they made the Alsatians yank out theirs from the slopes and put it down on the flat where the soil was common. Alsace, a regal place for wine, became known for the cheap stuff. When Alsace returned to France in 1919, replanting on better soils and slopes commenced. With World War II, there was a brief return to Germany once again. In 1945, back to France they went. Almost twenty years later, in 1962, they received appellation status. Amen.

They've been trying to get their crown back for a long time. Even now they are ignored, which is somehow inconceivable. After all, as Pascaline says 96% of a grape's success is having the right kind of sunlight and rain, the 4% is what lies underneath and what the farmer does with it. They have all three—the holy trinity.

The Dirt

The ribbon of the Alsace vineyard is in northeastern France in the shadows of Germany. It squiggles 60 miles between Strasbourg in the north to Mulhouse in the south. As I drove north through perfectly preserved medieval villages of half-timber, with their cascading red geraniums, I felt the shadows of the Vosges. Those granitic soldiers protect the region from western rains and make for one of the driest, sunniest climates in France with a variety of microclimates. To the east was Germany's Black Forest, and the Rhine. Those elements tell the soil's story.

Alsace seems made up of philosopher-vignerons and one of them is André Ostertag. He explained to me that at one time the Black Forest and the Vosges were one contiguous mountain range. Then calamity hit; its middle imploded. The collapsed part became the flat, rich soil excellent for planting anything but vines. But like Athena springing out of Zeus's head, the slopes of the Alsatian vineyards were born, just under what became those Vosges. The resulting soils were a cubist artwork of everything the Earth has to offer. Thirteen bedrocks, they said, a majority of which were limestone variations. And the others? Granite, gneiss, slate, schist, shale, basalt, gypsum, marl, volcanic variations, and sandstone.

Like Burgundy and Champagne, here too they believe in their Grands Crus vineyards. All are on the slopes, and they've identified 51 talented plots.

51 Named Vineyards Defined

Altenberg de Bergbieten	Marl-limestone-gypsum
Altenberg de Bergheim	Marl-limestone
Altenberg de Wolxheim	Marl-limestone
Brand (Turckheim)	Granite
Bruderthal (Molsheim)	Marl-limestone
Eichberg (Eguisheim)	Marl-limestone
Engelberg (Dahlenheim and Scharrachbergheim)	Marl-limestone
Florimont (Ingersheim and Katzenthal)	Marl-limestone
Frankstein (Dambach-la-ville)	Granite
Froehn (Zellenberg)	Clay-marl
Furstentum (Kientzheim and Sigolsheim)	Limestone
Geisberg (Ribeauvillé)	Marl-limestone-sandstone
Gloeckelberg (Rodern and Saint-Hippolyte)	Marl-limestone

Goldert (Gueberschwihr)	Marl-limestone
Hatschbourg (Hattstatt and Voegtlinshoffen)	Marl-limestone-loess
Hengst (Wintzenheim)	Marl-limestone-sandstone
Kaefferkopf (Ammerschwihr)	Granite-limestone-sandstone
Kanzlerberg (Bergheim)	Marl-clay-gypsum
Kastelberg (Andlau)	Shale
Kessler (Guebwiller)	Sandy-clay
Kirchberg de Barr	Marl-limestone
Kirchberg de Ribeauvillé	Marl-limestone-sandstone
Kitterlé (Guebwiller)	Sandstone-volcanic
Mambourg (Sigolsheim)	Marl-limestone
Mandelberg (Mittelwihr et Beblenheim)	Marl-limestone
Marckrain (Bennwihr et Sigolsheim)	Marl-limestone
Moenchberg (Andlau et Eichhoffen)	Marl-limestone-scree
Muenchberg (Nothalten)	Stony-sandstone-volcanic
Ollwiller (Wuenheim)	Sandy-clay
Osterberg (Ribeauvillé)	Marl
Pfersigberg (Eguisheim and Wettolsheim)	Limestone-sandstone
Pfingstberg (Orschwihr)	Marl-limestone-sandstone
Praelatenberg (Kientzheim)	Granitic
Rangen (Thann and Vieux-Thann)	Volcanic
Rosacker (Hunawihr)	Dolomitic limestone
Saering (Guebwiller)	Marl-limstone-sandstone

Schlossberg (Kientzheim)	Granitic
Schoenenbourg (Riquewihr and Zellenberg)	Marno-sableux-gypsum
Sommerberg (Niedermorschwihr and Katzenthal)	Granitic
Sonnenglanz (Beblenheim)	Marl-limestone
Spiegel (Bergholtz and Guebwiller)	Marl-sandstone
Sporen (Riquewihr)	Stony-clay-marl
Steinert (Pfaffenheim and Westhalten)	Limestone
Steingrubler (Wettolsheim)	Marl-limestone-sandstone
Steinklotz (Marlenheim)	Limestone
Vorbourg (Rouffach and Westhalten)	Limestone-sandstone
Wiebelsberg (Andlau)	Sandy-sandstone
Wineck-Schlossberg (Katzenthal and Ammerschwihr)	Granitic
Winzenberg (Blienschwiller)	Granitic
Zinnkoepflé (Soultzmatt and Westhalten)	Limestone-sandstone
Zotzenberg (Mittelbergheim)	Marl-limestone

The granite and the gneiss are mostly closest to the Vosges in the west. These soils have a coarse texture and low water retention. It is said that wines from those soils are expressive in their youth with an edgy structure. Schist is rare. There's only one Grand Cru based in it, Kastelberg, and that's up north in Andlau, where Domaine Kreydenweiss makes a great interpretation of it. Characteristics are broad in the mouth. Those basalts and granites? Some say they can bring a smoky (especially with Riesling) as well as oily textures. The most famous of their sandstones is the local pink (from iron) Gres des Vosges—just look at a picture of Strasbourg's pinkish cathedral to understand. They can be more shy, initially with a nervous acidity and bony structure. The variations on limestone change with what it's mixed with. More sand means a little more direct flavor. More clay means a firmer wine. More chalk—their famous is the fossil-laden muschelkalk and limestone, more verticality that is closed when young, the structure is broad with a lemon acidity

The Grapes

Before Alsace was known for the whites of today, it was known for red. Today just one, but notable, red grape is recognized to grow on their soil and that is Pinot Noir. As recently as 2012, the region didn't even mention it, they didn't want to promote it, saying that with only 10%, there wasn't enough. So it was our secret and it's a special one. The Pinot stays delicate yet deep, and there's nowhere else in the world where you can compare the grapes on limestone to schist to volcanic to sandstone in the same region. What fun. Some say the Pinot on limestone is more long-lived, on granite it is more fleshy in its youth. Pascaline thinks also that they have a distinctive smokiness, making them unique in a Pinot-soaked world.

For the white wines, there's the non-aromatic, almost neutral Sylvaner, Chasselas, Auxerrois, and Pinot Blanc. They are used in blends, and more and more for Crémant d'Alsace (except for Chasselas). With little exception, all are banned from Grand Cru hills. But the aromatic ones, these four grapes (as well as the Pinot Noir) are allowed on the exalted hills: Muscat, Gewurtztraminer, Pinot Gris, and their grand poobah, Riesling.

Muscat here is full of flower power and becomes a dry wine. The love it or leave it Gewürztraminer, with what can be, in various intensities, canned fruit salad, lemongrass, rose petal, and lychee, is not shy. Grow it in some of the subtropical zones of Alsace and it can beef up in alcohol and get oily and blowsy, making an interesting grape really hard to take with some quite bitter bones. They call it Pinot Grigio in Italy, Pinot Pinot Beurot in Burgundy, and in Alsace, it's Pinot Gris, and a different animal. There it shows up as exotically spiced, like some Thai dessert, and can zoom up to a high alcohol if you turn your back. It shows up in everything from sweet to dry wine. This is the land of solar power and to really express the grape it needs to struggle on poor soils, like granite that preserves the grape's acidity. Or, as André Ostertag said to me, "Pinot Gris expresses the soil in his corpulence. But with age Pinot Gris shows great tannic structure, so it can almost behave like a red wine."

But without a doubt this is Riesling country. And it's sensitive. Ostertag said, "Riesling is a sponge of the soil much more capable in capturing the subtleties." The Alsatian Riesling rarely has the delicacy of the cold and wet climate of the Mosel. Here it is fuller and historically drier, and it has no trouble fermenting all of its sugars. The grape expresses itself in every style of wine, from bubbles to the super-sweet wines called Sélection de Grains Nobles and Vendage Tardives, the Alsatian equivalent of of the German Sweet wines, BA/TBA. You'll find winemakers duking it out as to which soils give the best expression. Is it true that here the limestone and chalk take it all or does the salty, mineral edge of granite succeed? You choose.

In the past, Alsace was a glorious garden of grapes and field blends, and there are two categories of wines that pay homage to the region's history. The label Gentil is required to have a minimum of 50% Riesling, Muscat, and/or Gewürztraminer, Pinot Gris, with the rest made up of Sylvaner, Chasselas, and/or Pinot Blanc. Before blending, each grape variety must be vinified separately and must officially qualify as AOC. Edelzwicker is the other common label, and it is used to indicate any blended wine. Unlike Gentil, the law doesn't require certain grape varieties or amounts. And when Pinot Blanc is mixed with Auxerrois, the blend is called Klevner.

THE ALSATIAN REVOLUTION:
IT'S THE PLACE, NOT THE GRAPE

Alsace has one of the oldest traditions of bottling under the grape name. This probably came from German influence, as there are no early French examples of this. In 2000, Jean-Michel Deiss said, enough. He bottled a blend from each vineyard. The world gasped. It was so very counter to modern Alsace and the world where terroir was defined as one grape, one place. Yet, while blends were historically common in the area, you just did not do this on Grand Cru.

Deiss is no longer alone. Others have gone the route of eliminating the variety pronouncement on the label on some of the wines, trying to push the message of place not grape. In other regions of France there would be punishment. But in tolerant Alsace? Not so.

Alsace remains a place that clings to freedom and has fostered many independent thinkers, like Meyer. This is a region that fails to be narrowed into one idea, or one soil type. Twenty percent of the land is organic—a huge percentage—and there are a tremendous number of those working in edgy ways, yet being relatively conservative and dedicated. And where others might be kicked out of the appellation for tasting against the mainstream, or planting where they shouldn't—as they do in Burgundy and the Loire, Alsace is very tolerant and inclusive. Why is a good question. Perhaps it's because they've lost their land so often they are sensitive to the idea that if you work well, if you respect the Earth, then that's what matters.

In this sunny region with the crazy soils, the wine range is immense, well-priced, and strongly terroir driven. The region is filled with philosophers and thinkers, and as I took my leave of Ostertag I asked him about the conflict in the world about whether the taste of the soils can translate into the grape. He answered, "I am not a scientist. As a winemaker I act more as a poet. My poetic sensibility tells me that we human beings are what goes through us, passes through us, and nourishes us. I do not see how it could it be different for the vines."

WHO TO DRINK

- Domaine Schueller (organic)
- Domaine Frick (biodynamic)
- Domaine Christian Binner (biodynamic)
- Les Vins Pirouettes par Binner (organic. biodynamic)
- Domaine Josmeyer (biodynamic)
- Domaine Barmès Buecher (biodynamic)
- Domaine Dirler-Cadé (biodynamic)
- Domaine Zind-Humbrecht (biodynamic)
- Domaine Kreydenweiss (biodynamic)
- Catherine Riss (biodynamic)
- Domaine Julien Meyer (biodynamic)
- Domaine Ostertag (biodynamic)
- Domaine Léon Boesch (organic)
- Domaine Fritsch (organicl)
- Domaine Valentin Zusslin (biodynamic)
- Domaine Marcel Deiss (biodynamic)
- Domaine J-L. Trapet (biodynamic)
- La Grange de l'Oncle Charles (organic)
- Vignoble du Rêveur/Mathieu Deiss (biodynamic)
- Domaine Weinbach (biodynamic)
- Domaine Laurent Barth (biodynamic)

CLOSING NOTE

This is not meant to be an encyclopedia, but rather an exploration of the places that make the wines we love best. So if your favorite wine region isn't here, we hope this book will arm you with the tools and the questions to go forth and find the answers and the tastes yourself. Hopefully this will set you on your way. If there's one thing writing this book has taught us, it is that the more we know, the more we don't.

ACKNOWLEDGMENTS

The Dirty Guide to Wine grew from an editor who told me, "We don't want a memoir about a serial killer, we want a beginner's wine book," I admit. I took it as a dare.

So there we go, a beginner's guide based on bedrock. To my shock, a fabulous publisher wanted it. Thanks to Dan Crissman of Countryman for his enthusiasm and vision. Actually, Norton has been great, from Dan to the finishing editor Róisín Cameron and everyone else in between from—design to copy to publicity—this imprint been a joy to work with.

I am a weakling without cheerleaders, and lucky for me, I've had them. As always, a thank you to Melissa Clark for her years of support. A particularly big thank you to the super-bright and lovable chief editor of Punch.com, Talia Baiocchi, for being an ardent and early enthusiast of this idea. Jose Pastor, my co-loving granite friend, xoxo. To my writing comrade, Sue Shapiro, even though I was barred from bringing this non-narrative in on our Thursday nights, I swear, you were sitting over my shoulder giving guidance. #onemorewinebook.

I'll fess up: this book was an extremely difficult undertaking. In fact, the subtitle of this book should be, *the more you know, the more you don't know*. Wine and how it becomes magic is a very complicated web. As neither a geologist nor a soil scientist nor an adept winemaker, I would

not have been able to cross the finish line without the help and author-
ity of those who actually work the dirt and the vine. There were so many
that I hope I don't leave someone out, but if your name isn't here, it's in
my heart. Guy Bossard and Jo Landron in the Muscadet. Pierre Breton in
Bourgeuil. Damien Delechenau in Montlouis. Kenji Hodgson and Richard Leroy in Faye D'Anjou. Andre Ostertag, Patrick Meyer, and Christian
Binner in Alsace. Eric Texier in Charnay. Jean Foillard in Fleurie. Olivier
de Moor in Chablis. Jean Claude Rateau, Claire Naudin, Jean-Yves Bizot,
and Aubert de Villaine in Burgundy. Bertrand Gautherot in Champagne.
Salvo Foti in Sicily on Mount Etna, Mattia and Odilio Antonioto in Bramaterra, and Frances Fogarty in Boca. Maria José and Julio César López
de Heredia and Jesús Madrazo in Rioja. Jason Lett in Oregon. Merci.
Grazie. Gracias. Thank you. Your help, patience, and enthusiasm were
water to my vine.

I want to send a thank you to Pedro Parra of Chile who spends a lot
of this time thinking about the issues in this book. And to Dr. Kevin
R. Pogue of Whitman College. What can I say. To you I offer the most
intense and humble thank you. Dr. Pogue did his best to bring me up to
speed as fast as he could. He was free with his red pen and his anger at
my ignorance, and I drank up every correction with gratefulness.

If there are any mistakes in the book, please know that he did his
best to prevent them. Any flubs or missteps here are totally our own.
And to the professor: I am forever cured of the sloppy habit of using
the word soils to describe what are actually bedrocks, and I am hoping,
because of your help, this book stops everyone who has been guilty of
that in the past as well. I look forward to drinking some wine grown
over the influence of basalt bedrock with you one day soon.

Finally, a thank you to Pasacaline Lepeltier. Pascaline and I met in
2007 in Paris and as soon as she relocated to the United States, she
quickly became ma fille francaise, my French daughter. Without a doubt,
this would be a very different book without her participation. I relied

on her vast knowledge, her ability to analyze taste, and her insanely brilliant ability for fact retention. A major talent, she was my personal encyclopedia, and managed to multi-task even as she was in the throes of opening a restaurant and the not-so-fresh-hell that comes with. I learned so much from you on the way. PP, thank you for the journey.

INDEX

Sancerre, 110, 148, 152, 174, 187
sand, 30
sandstone, 109–10; and Alsace,
    227–30; and Barolo, 160, 166;
    and Brouilly, 97; and Gres des
    Vosges, 229; and Jura, 133; and
    Kamptal, 218; and Les Noëls de
    Montbenault, 197; and Sedimen-
    tary Cheat Sheet, 187
Sangiovese, 176, 185–87
Santa Rita Hills vineyard, 110, 176,
    182, 187
Santana, Roberto, 62, 206
Saône, 114, 132
Sauternais, and gravels, 178
Sauternes, 152, 178
Sauvignon Blanc: and Burgundy,
    119; and Cabernet Sauvignon,
    181; and Entre-Deux-Mers, 178;
    and gravels, 178; and Sedimen-
    tary Cheat Sheet, 186–87; and
    shale, 177; and silex, 174–75; and
    Touraine, 149
Sauvignon Gris, 181
Savagnin, 133–36, 186
Savennières, and schist, 194, 200
schiefer, 190, 215
schist, 190–99; and Alsace, 227,
    229, 230; and Anjou Noir, 157;
    and Banyuls, 204–5; and Chenin
    Blanc, 201; and Chenin, 15; and
    Collioure, 204–5; and Côte-Rôte,
    73, 80, 82–83; and Faugères, 203–
    4; and Francesca Padovani, 176;
    and Galicia, 209; and Goulaine,
    93; and Igneous Cheat Sheet,
    108; and Juliénas, 97; and Jura,
    132; and Kastelberg, 229; and
    Languedoc-Roussillon, 202; and
    Léon Barral, 221; and Metamor-
    phic Cheat Sheet, 222, 223; and
    Mosel, 66, 214–17; and Muscadet,
    88; and Ribeira Sacra, 208, 212,

213; and Richard Leroy, 221; and
    Savennières, 194, 200; and Sedi-
    mentary Cheat Sheet, 187
schistes gréseux, 194, 204, 212
Science Life, 24
Scirto, Giuseppe, 58, 60
Sélection de Grains Nobles, 231
Sémillon, 181, 187
Serine, 77
shale, 109, 110, 175–77; and Alsace,
    227, 228; and apples, 32; and
    Campi di Fonterenza, 185; and
    Finger Lakes, 216; and hornfels
    190; and Julien Labet, 133; and
    David Lett, 64; and Loire, 193;
    and Les Noëls de Montbenault,
    197; and Ribeira Sacra, 208; and
    Santa Cruz, 117; and Sedimen-
    tary Cheat Sheet, 187
Shaw Vineyard, 175
Sherry, and diatomaceous rock, 183
silex, 110, 151–52, 174–75, 184, 187
silica, 194, 211; and diatomite, 110,
    182; and loess, 31; and sand, 30;
    and schistes gréseux, 194; and
    teas, 35; and tuff, 66, 68
silicon dioxide, 110
silt, 31
Sizzano, 67
slate, 190, 191, 208; and Alsace, 227,
    232; and Anjou, 195, 198; Devo-
    nian, 215; and Galicia, 205–6;
    and Immich-Batterieberg, 221;
    and Loire, 194; and Metamor-
    phic Cheat Sheet, 222–23; and
    Mosel, 214–17; and potash, 208;
    and rain, 212
Soldera, and shale, 176
Sorrenberg, 98
Souhaut, Hervé, 73, 106
Sousón, 210
Souzay-Champigny, 157
Spanna. See Nebbiola

Twain, Mark, 139
Typhon, 54

U
Ugni Blanc, 181
Ull de Llebre, 172
Uva Rara, 70, 108

V
Valdespino, 183
Valette, Philippe, 131
Valette wines, 131
Vallana Spanna, 68, 71
Valsesia, 68
Van Berg, Bernard, 122–25, 127
Vendage Tardives, 231
"*vent du Midi*," 130
Vermont, 23
vertical structure, 40
Vespolina, 70
Veuve Clicquot, soil of, 28
Vigna, 167
Villaine, Aubert de, 32–33, 130
Villaine, Pamela de, 130
Vin de France, 119, 124
vin de soif, 58, 149
Vin Jaune, 134–36
vin mousseux, 142
Vinho Verde, 209

Vinos Atlánticos, 207. *See also* Atlantic Wines
Viognier, 73, 77, 80, 83, 107, 150
"vital impetus," 17
voile, 134
volatile acidity, 47
Vosges, 226–27, 229
Vosne Les Jachées, 121
Vosne-Romanée, 32, 119, 126
Vouvray, 149, 151–53; and silex, 174–75

W
Walla Walla, 30, 31, 52
Wasserman, Sheldon, 163
Weissburgunder, 216
Wiemer, Hermann J., 175
Willamette Valley, 63–65, 108
Wine & Spirits, 21
Wine Advocate, The, 98
Wine Grapes (Robinson), 70, 77
Winebow, 168
Wurdeman, John, 18

Y
Year Book of French Quality Wines, Spirits, & Liquors, 154

Z
Zweigelt, and gneiss, 218